DEATH OF A SALESMAN

Arthur Miller

SPARK PUBLISHING

SPARKNOTES is a registered trademark of SparkNotes LLC

Spark Publishing
A Division of Barnes & Noble
120 Fifth Avenue
New York, NY 10011
www.sparknotes.com

ISBN-13: 978-1-4114-0368-0
ISBN-10: 1-4114-0368-1

Please submit changes or report errors to www.sparknotes.com/errors.

Printed in the United States.

10 9 8 7 6 5 4

CONTENTS

CONTEXT

ARTHUR MILLER WAS BORN in New York City on October 17, 1915. His career as a playwright began while he was a student at the University of Michigan. Several of his early works won prizes, and during his senior year, the Federal Theatre Project in Detroit performed one of his works. He produced his first great success, *All My Sons,* in 1947. Two years later, Miller wrote *Death of a Salesman,* which won the Pulitzer Prize and transformed Miller into a national sensation. Many critics described *Death of a Salesman* as the first great American tragedy, and Miller gained eminence as a man who understood the deep essence of the United States. He published *The Crucible* in 1953, a searing indictment of the anti-Communist hysteria that pervaded 1950s America. He has won the New York Drama Critics Circle Award twice, and his *Broken Glass* (1993) won the Olivier Award for Best Play of the London Season.

Death of a Salesman, Miller's most famous work, addresses the painful conflicts within one family, but it also tackles larger issues regarding American national values. The play examines the cost of blind faith in the American Dream. In this respect, it offers a postwar American reading of personal tragedy in the tradition of Sophocles' *Oedipus Cycle.* Miller charges America with selling a false myth constructed around a capitalist materialism nurtured by the postwar economy, a materialism that obscured the personal truth and moral vision of the original American Dream described by the country's founders.

A half century after it was written, *Death of a Salesman* remains a powerful drama. Its indictment of fundamental American values and the American Dream of material success may seem somewhat tame in today's age of constant national and individual self-analysis and criticism, but its challenge was quite radical for its time. After World War II, the United States faced profound and irreconcilable domestic tensions and contradictions. Although the war had ostensibly engendered an unprecedented sense of American confidence, prosperity, and security, the United States became increasingly embroiled in a tense cold war with the Soviet Union. The propagation of myths of a peaceful, homogenous, and nauseatingly gleeful American golden age was tempered by constant anxiety about

Communism, bitter racial conflict, and largely ignored economic and social stratification. Many Americans could not subscribe to the degree of social conformity and the ideological and cultural orthodoxy that a prosperous, booming, conservative suburban middle-class championed.

Uneasy with this American milieu of denial and discord, a new generation of artists and writers influenced by existentialist philosophy and the hypocritical postwar condition took up arms in a battle for self-realization and expression of personal meaning. Such discontented individuals railed against capitalist success as the basis of social approval, disturbed that so many American families centered their lives around material possessions (cars, appliances, and especially the just-introduced television)—often in an attempt to keep up with their equally materialistic neighbors. The climate of the American art world had likewise long been stuck in its own rut of conformity, confusion, and disorder following the prewar climax of European Modernism and the wake of assorted -isms associated with modern art and literature. The notions of Sigmund Freud and Carl Jung regarding the role of the human subconscious in defining and accepting human existence, coupled with the existentialist concern with the individual's responsibility for understanding one's existence on one's own terms, captivated the imaginations of postwar artists and writers. Perhaps the most famous and widely read dramatic work associated with existentialist philosophy is Samuel Beckett's *Waiting for Godot*. Miller fashioned a particularly American version of the European existentialist stance, incorporating and playing off idealistic notions of success and individuality specific to the United States.

The basis for the dramatic conflict in *Death of a Salesman* lies in Arthur Miller's conflicted relationship with his uncle, Manny Newman, also a salesman. Newman imagined a continuous competition between his son and Miller. Newman refused to accept failure and demanded the appearance of utmost confidence in his household. In his youth, Miller had written a short story about an unsuccessful salesman. His relationship with Manny revived his interest in the abandoned manuscript. He transformed the story into one of the most successful dramas in the history of the American stage. In expressing the emotions that Manny Newman inspired through the fictional character of Willy Loman, Miller managed to touch deep chords within the national psyche.

Plot Overview

AS A FLUTE MELODY PLAYS, Willy Loman returns to his home in Brooklyn one night, exhausted from a failed sales trip. His wife, Linda, tries to persuade him to ask his boss, Howard Wagner, to let him work in New York so that he won't have to travel. Willy says that he will talk to Howard the next day. Willy complains that Biff, his older son who has come back home to visit, has yet to make something of himself. Linda scolds Willy for being so critical, and Willy goes to the kitchen for a snack.

As Willy talks to himself in the kitchen, Biff and his younger brother, Happy, who is also visiting, reminisce about their adolescence and discuss their father's babbling, which often includes criticism of Biff's failure to live up to Willy's expectations. As Biff and Happy, dissatisfied with their lives, fantasize about buying a ranch out West, Willy becomes immersed in a daydream. He praises his sons, now younger, who are washing his car. The young Biff, a high school football star, and the young Happy appear. They interact affectionately with their father, who has just returned from a business trip. Willy confides in Biff and Happy that he is going to open his own business one day, bigger than that owned by his neighbor, Charley. Charley's son, Bernard, enters looking for Biff, who must study for math class in order to avoid failing. Willy points out to his sons that although Bernard is smart, he is not "well liked," which will hurt him in the long run.

A younger Linda enters, and the boys leave to do some chores. Willy boasts of a phenomenally successful sales trip, but Linda coaxes him into revealing that his trip was actually only meagerly successful. Willy complains that he soon won't be able to make all of the payments on their appliances and car. He complains that people don't like him and that he's not good at his job. As Linda consoles him, he hears the laughter of his mistress. He approaches The Woman, who is still laughing, and engages in another reminiscent daydream. Willy and The Woman flirt, and she thanks him for giving her stockings.

The Woman disappears, and Willy fades back into his prior daydream, in the kitchen. Linda, now mending stockings, reassures him. He scolds her mending and orders her to throw the stockings out. Bernard bursts in, again looking for Biff. Linda reminds Willy that Biff has to return a football that he stole, and she adds that Biff is too rough with the neighborhood girls. Willy hears The Woman laugh and explodes at Bernard and Linda. Both leave, and though the daydream ends, Willy continues to mutter to himself. The older Happy comes downstairs and tries to quiet Willy. Agitated, Willy shouts his regret about not going to Alaska with his brother, Ben, who eventually found a diamond mine in Africa and became rich. Charley, having heard the commotion, enters. Happy goes off to bed, and Willy and Charley begin to play cards. Charley offers Willy a job, but Willy, insulted, refuses it. As they argue, Willy imagines that Ben enters. Willy accidentally calls Charley Ben. Ben inspects Willy's house and tells him that he has to catch a train soon to look at properties in Alaska. As Willy talks to Ben about the prospect of going to Alaska, Charley, seeing no one there, gets confused and questions Willy. Willy yells at Charley, who leaves. The younger Linda enters and Ben meets her. Willy asks Ben impatiently about his life. Ben recounts his travels and talks about their father. As Ben is about to leave, Willy daydreams further, and Charley and Bernard rush in to tell him that Biff and Happy are stealing lumber. Although Ben eventually leaves, Willy continues to talk to him.

Back in the present, the older Linda enters to find Willy outside. Biff and Happy come downstairs and discuss Willy's condition with their mother. Linda scolds Biff for judging Willy harshly. Biff tells her that he knows Willy is a fake, but he refuses to elaborate. Linda mentions that Willy has tried to commit suicide. Happy grows angry and rebukes Biff for his failure in the business world. Willy enters and yells at Biff. Happy intervenes and eventually proposes that he and Biff go into the sporting goods business together. Willy immediately brightens and gives Biff a host of tips about asking for a loan from one of Biff's old employers, Bill Oliver. After more arguing and reconciliation, everyone finally goes to bed.

Act II opens with Willy enjoying the breakfast that Linda has made for him. Willy ponders the bright-seeming future before getting angry again about his expensive appliances. Linda informs Willy that Biff and Happy are taking him out to dinner that night. Excited, Willy announces that he is going to make Howard Wagner give him a New York job. The phone rings, and Linda chats with Biff, reminding him to be nice to his father at the restaurant that night.

As the lights fade on Linda, they come up on Howard playing with a wire recorder in his office. Willy tries to broach the subject of working in New York, but Howard interrupts him and makes him listen to his kids and wife on the wire recorder. When Willy finally gets a word in, Howard rejects his plea. Willy launches into a lengthy recalling of how a legendary salesman named Dave Single- man inspired him to go into sales. Howard leaves and Willy gets angry. Howard soon re-enters and tells Willy to take some time off. Howard leaves and Ben enters, inviting Willy to join him in Alaska. The younger Linda enters and reminds Willy of his sons and job. The young Biff enters, and Willy praises Biff's prospects and the fact that he is well liked.

Ben leaves and Bernard rushes in, eagerly awaiting Biff's big football game. Willy speaks optimistically to Biff about the game. Charley enters and teases Willy about the game. As Willy chases Charley off, the lights rise on a different part of the stage. Willy continues yelling from offstage, and Jenny, Charley's secretary, asks a grown-up Bernard to quiet him down. Willy enters and prattles on about a "very big deal" that Biff is working on. Daunted by Bernard's success (he mentions to Willy that he is going to Wash- ington to fight a case), Willy asks Bernard why Biff turned out to be such a failure. Bernard asks Willy what happened in Boston that made Biff decide not to go to summer school. Willy defensively tells Bernard not to blame him.

Charley enters and sees Bernard off. When Willy asks for more money than Charley usually loans him, Charley again offers Willy a job. Willy again refuses and eventually tells Charley that he was fired. Charley scolds Willy for always needing to be liked and an- grily gives him the money. Calling Charley his only friend, Willy exits on the verge of tears.

At Frank's Chop House, Happy helps Stanley, a waiter, prepare a table. They ogle and chat up a girl, Miss Forsythe, who enters the restaurant. Biff enters, and Happy introduces him to Miss Forsythe, continuing to flirt with her. Miss Forsythe, a call girl, leaves to tele- phone another call girl (at Happy's request), and Biff spills out that he waited six hours for Bill Oliver and Oliver didn't even recognize him. Upset at his father's unrelenting misconception that he, Biff, was a salesman for Oliver, Biff plans to relieve Willy of his illusions. Willy enters, and Biff tries gently, at first, to tell him what happened at Oliver's office. Willy blurts out that he was fired. Stunned, Biff again tries to let Willy down easily. Happy cuts in with remarks sug- gesting Biff's success, and Willy eagerly awaits the good news.

Biff finally explodes at Willy for being unwilling to listen. The young Bernard runs in shouting for Linda, and Biff, Happy, and Willy start to argue. As Biff explains what happened, their conversation recedes into the background. The young Bernard tells Linda that Biff failed math. The restaurant conversation comes back into focus and Willy criticizes Biff for failing math. Willy then hears the voice of the hotel operator in Boston and shouts that he is not in his room. Biff scrambles to quiet Willy and claims that Oliver is talking to his partner about giving Biff the money. Willy's renewed interest and probing questions irk Biff more, and he screams at Willy. Willy hears The Woman laugh and he shouts back at Biff, hitting him and staggering. Miss Forsythe enters with another call girl, Letta. Biff helps Willy to the washroom and, finding Happy flirting with the girls, argues with him about Willy. Biff storms out, and Happy follows with the girls.

Willy and The Woman enter, dressing themselves and flirting. The door knocks and Willy hurries The Woman into the bathroom. Willy answers the door; the young Biff enters and tells Willy that he failed math. Willy tries to usher him out of the room, but Biff imitates his math teacher's lisp, which elicits laughter from Willy and The Woman. Willy tries to cover up his indiscretion, but Biff refuses to believe his stories and storms out, dejected, calling Willy a "phony little fake." Back in the restaurant, Stanley helps Willy up. Willy asks him where he can find a seed store. Stanley gives him directions to one, and Willy hurries off.

The light comes up on the Loman kitchen, where Happy enters looking for Willy. He moves into the living room and sees Linda. Biff comes inside and Linda scolds the boys and slaps away the flowers in Happy's hand. She yells at them for abandoning Willy. Happy attempts to appease her, but Biff goes in search of Willy. He finds Willy planting seeds in the garden with a flashlight. Willy is consulting Ben about a $20,000 proposition. Biff approaches him to say goodbye and tries to bring him inside. Willy moves into the house, followed by Biff, and becomes angry again about Biff's failure. Happy tries to calm Biff, but Biff and Willy erupt in fury at each other. Biff starts to sob, which touches Willy. Everyone goes to bed except Willy, who renews his conversation with Ben, elated at how great Biff will be with $20,000 of insurance money. Linda soon calls out for Willy but gets no response. Biff and Happy listen as well. They hear Willy's car speed away.

In the requiem, Linda and Happy stand in shock after Willy's poorly attended funeral. Biff states that Willy had the wrong dreams. Charley defends Willy as a victim of his profession. Ready to leave, Biff invites Happy to go back out West with him. Happy declares that he will stick it out in New York to validate Willy's death. Linda asks Willy for forgiveness for being unable to cry. She begins to sob, repeating "We're free. . . ." All exit, and the flute melody is heard as the curtain falls.

Character List

Willy Loman An insecure, self-deluded traveling salesman. Willy believes wholeheartedly in the American Dream of easy success and wealth, but he never achieves it. Nor do his sons fulfill his hope that they will succeed where he has failed. When Willy's illusions begin to fail under the pressing realities of his life, his mental health begins to unravel. The overwhelming tensions caused by this disparity, as well as those caused by the societal imperatives that drive Willy, form the essential conflict of *Death of a Salesman*.

Biff Loman Willy's thirty-four-year-old elder son. Biff led a charmed life in high school as a football star with scholarship prospects, good male friends, and fawning female admirers. He failed math, however, and did not have enough credits to graduate. Since then, his kleptomania has gotten him fired from every job that he has held. Biff represents Willy's vulnerable, poetic, tragic side. He cannot ignore his instincts, which tell him to abandon Willy's paralyzing dreams and move out West to work with his hands. He ultimately fails to reconcile his life with Willy's expectations of him.

Linda Loman Willy's loyal, loving wife. Linda suffers through Willy's grandiose dreams and self-delusions. Occasionally, she seems to be taken in by Willy's self-deluded hopes for future glory and success, but at other times, she seems far more realistic and less fragile than her husband. She has nurtured the family through all of Willy's misguided attempts at success, and her emotional strength and perseverance support Willy until his collapse.

Happy Loman Willy's thirty-two-year-old younger son. Happy has lived in Biff's shadow all of his life, but he compensates by nurturing his relentless sex drive and professional ambition. Happy represents Willy's sense of self-importance, ambition, and blind servitude to societal expectations. Although he works as an assistant to an assistant buyer in a department store, Happy presents himself as supremely important. Additionally, he practices bad business ethics and sleeps with the girlfriends of his superiors.

Charley Willy's next-door neighbor. Charley owns a successful business and his son, Bernard, is a wealthy, important lawyer. Willy is jealous of Charley's success. Charley gives Willy money to pay his bills, and Willy reveals at one point, choking back tears, that Charley is his only friend.

Bernard Bernard is Charley's son and an important, successful lawyer. Although Willy used to mock Bernard for studying hard, Bernard always loved Willy's sons dearly and regarded Biff as a hero. Bernard's success is difficult for Willy to accept because his own sons' lives do not measure up.

Ben Willy's wealthy older brother. Ben has recently died and appears only in Willy's "daydreams." Willy regards Ben as a symbol of the success that he so desperately craves for himself and his sons.

The Woman Willy's mistress when Happy and Biff were in high school. The Woman's attention and admiration boost Willy's fragile ego. When Biff catches Willy in his hotel room with The Woman, he loses faith in his father, and his dream of passing math and going to college dies.

Howard Wagner Willy's boss. Howard inherited the company from his father, whom Willy regarded as "a masterful man" and "a prince." Though much younger than Willy, Howard treats Willy with condescension and eventually fires him, despite Willy's wounded assertions that he named Howard at his birth.

Stanley   A waiter at Frank's Chop House. Stanley and Happy seem to be friends, or at least acquaintances, and they banter about and ogle Miss Forsythe together before Biff and Willy arrive at the restaurant.

Miss Forsythe and Letta Two young women whom Happy and Biff meet at Frank's Chop House. It seems likely that Miss Forsythe and Letta are prostitutes, judging from Happy's repeated comments about their moral character and the fact that they are "on call."

Jenny   Charley's secretary.

ANALYSIS OF MAJOR CHARACTERS

WILLY LOMAN

Despite his desperate searching through his past, Willy does not achieve the self-realization or self-knowledge typical of the tragic hero. The quasi-resolution that his suicide offers him represents only a partial discovery of the truth. While he achieves a professional understanding of himself and the fundamental nature of the sales profession, Willy fails to realize his personal failure and betrayal of his soul and family through the meticulously constructed artifice of his life. He cannot grasp the true personal, emotional, spiritual understanding of himself as a literal "loman" or "low man." Willy is too driven by his own "willy"-ness or perverse "willfulness" to recognize the slanted reality that his desperate mind has forged. Still, many critics, focusing on Willy's entrenchment in a quagmire of lies, delusions, and self-deceptions, ignore the significant accomplishment of his partial self-realization. Willy's failure to recognize the anguished love offered to him by his family is crucial to the climax of his torturous day, and the play presents this incapacity as the real tragedy. Despite this failure, Willy makes the most extreme sacrifice in his attempt to leave an inheritance that will allow Biff to fulfill the American Dream.

Ben's final mantra—"The jungle is dark, but full of diamonds"— turns Willy's suicide into a metaphorical moral struggle, a final skewed ambition to realize his full commercial and material capacity. His final act, according to Ben, is "not like an appointment at all" but like a "diamond . . . rough and hard to the touch." In the absence of any real degree of self-knowledge or truth, Willy is able to achieve a tangible result. In some respect, Willy does experience a sort of revelation, as he finally comes to understand that the product he sells is himself. Through the imaginary advice of Ben, Willy ends up fully believing his earlier assertion to Charley that "after all the highways, and the trains, and the appointments, and the years, you end up worth more dead than alive."

BIFF LOMAN

Unlike Willy and Happy, Biff feels compelled to seek the truth about himself. While his father and brother are unable to accept the miserable reality of their respective lives, Biff acknowledges his failure and eventually manages to confront it. Even the difference between his name and theirs reflects this polarity: whereas Willy and Happy willfully and happily delude themselves, Biff bristles stiffly at self-deception. Biff's discovery that Willy has a mistress strips him of his faith in Willy and Willy's ambitions for him. Consequently, Willy sees Biff as an underachiever, while Biff sees himself as trapped in Willy's grandiose fantasies. After his epiphany in Bill Oliver's office, Biff determines to break through the lies surrounding the Loman family in order to come to realistic terms with his own life. Intent on revealing the simple and humble truth behind Willy's fantasy, Biff longs for the territory (the symbolically free West) obscured by his father's blind faith in a skewed, materialist version of the American Dream. Biff's identity crisis is a function of his and his father's disillusionment, which, in order to reclaim his identity, he must expose.

HAPPY LOMAN

Happy shares none of the poetry that erupts from Biff and that is buried in Willy—he is the stunted incarnation of Willy's worst traits and the embodiment of the lie of the happy American Dream. As such, Happy is a difficult character with whom to empathize. He is one-dimensional and static throughout the play. His empty vow to avenge Willy's death by finally "beat[ing] this racket" provides evidence of his critical condition: for Happy, who has lived in the shadow of the inflated expectations of his brother, there is no escape from the Dream's indoctrinated lies. Happy's diseased condition is irreparable—he lacks even the tiniest spark of self-knowledge or capacity for self-analysis. He does share Willy's capacity for self-delusion, trumpeting himself as the assistant buyer at his store, when, in reality, he is only an assistant to the assistant buyer. He does not possess a hint of the latent thirst for knowledge that proves Biff's salvation. Happy is a doomed, utterly duped figure, destined to be swallowed up by the force of blind ambition that fuels his insatiable sex drive.

Linda Loman and Charley

Linda and Charley serve as forces of reason throughout the play. Linda is probably the most enigmatic and complex character in *Death of a Salesman,* or even in all of Miller's work. Linda views freedom as an escape from debt, the reward of total ownership of the material goods that symbolize success and stability. Willy's prolonged obsession with the American Dream seems, over the long years of his marriage, to have left Linda internally conflicted. Nevertheless, Linda, by far the toughest, most realistic, and most level-headed character in the play, appears to have kept her emotional life intact. As such, she represents the emotional core of the drama.

If Linda is a sort of emotional prophet, overcome by the inevitable end that she foresees with startling clarity, then Charley functions as a sort of poetic prophet or sage. Miller portrays Charley as ambiguously gendered or effeminate, much like Tiresias, the mythological seer in Sophocles' *Oedipus* plays. Whereas Linda's lucid diagnosis of Willy's rapid decline is made possible by her emotional sanity, Charley's prognosis of the situation is logical, grounded firmly in practical reasoned analysis. He recognizes Willy's financial failure, and the job offer that he extends to Willy constitutes a common-sense solution. Though he is not terribly fond of Willy, Charley understands his plight and shields him from blame.

THEMES, MOTIFS & SYMBOLS

THEMES

Themes are the fundamental and often universal ideas explored in a literary work.

THE AMERICAN DREAM

Willy believes wholeheartedly in what he considers the promise of the American Dream—that a "well liked" and "personally attractive" man in business will indubitably and deservedly acquire the material comforts offered by modern American life. Oddly, his fixation with the superficial qualities of attractiveness and likeability is at odds with a more gritty, more rewarding understanding of the American Dream that identifies hard work without complaint as the key to success. Willy's interpretation of likeability is superficial—he childishly dislikes Bernard because he considers Bernard a nerd. Willy's blind faith in his stunted version of the American Dream leads to his rapid psychological decline when he is unable to accept the disparity between the Dream and his own life.

ABANDONMENT

Willy's life charts a course from one abandonment to the next, leaving him in greater despair each time. Willy's father leaves him and Ben when Willy is very young, leaving Willy neither a tangible (money) nor an intangible (history) legacy. Ben eventually departs for Alaska, leaving Willy to lose himself in a warped vision of the American Dream. Likely a result of these early experiences, Willy develops a fear of abandonment, which makes him want his family to conform to the American Dream. His efforts to raise perfect sons, however, reflect his inability to understand reality. The young Biff, whom Willy considers the embodiment of promise, drops Willy and Willy's zealous ambitions for him when he finds out about Willy's adultery. Biff's ongoing inability to succeed in business furthers his estrangement from Willy. When, at Frank's Chop House, Willy finally believes that Biff is on the cusp of greatness, Biff shatters Willy's illusions and, along with Happy, abandons the deluded, babbling Willy in the washroom.

BETRAYAL

Willy's primary obsession throughout the play is what he considers to be Biff's betrayal of his ambitions for him. Willy believes that he has every right to expect Biff to fulfill the promise inherent in him. When Biff walks out on Willy's ambitions for him, Willy takes this rejection as a personal affront (he associates it with "insult" and "spite"). Willy, after all, is a salesman, and Biff's ego-crushing rebuff ultimately reflects Willy's inability to sell him on the American Dream—the product in which Willy himself believes most faithfully. Willy assumes that Biff's betrayal stems from Biff's discovery of Willy's affair with The Woman—a betrayal of Linda's love. Whereas Willy feels that Biff has betrayed him, Biff feels that Willy, a "phony little fake," has betrayed *him* with his unending stream of ego-stroking lies.

MOTIFS

Motifs are recurring structures, contrasts, and literary devices that can help to develop and inform the text's major themes.

MYTHIC FIGURES

Willy's tendency to mythologize people contributes to his deluded understanding of the world. He speaks of Dave Singleman as a legend and imagines that his death must have been beautifully noble. Willy compares Biff and Happy to the mythic Greek figures Adonis and Hercules because he believes that his sons are pinnacles of "personal attractiveness" and power through "well liked"-ness; to him, they seem the very incarnation of the American Dream.

Willy's mythologizing proves quite nearsighted, however. Willy fails to realize the hopelessness of Singleman's lonely, on-the-job, on-the-road death. Trying to achieve what he considers to be Singleman's heroic status, Willy commits himself to a pathetic death and meaningless legacy (even if Willy's life insurance policy ends up paying off, Biff wants nothing to do with Willy's ambition for him). Similarly, neither Biff nor Happy ends up leading an ideal, godlike life; while Happy does believe in the American Dream, it seems likely that he will end up no better off than the decidedly ungodlike Willy.

THE AMERICAN WEST, ALASKA, AND THE AFRICAN JUNGLE

These regions represent the potential of instinct to Biff and Willy. Willy's father found success in Alaska and his brother, Ben, became rich in Africa; these exotic locales, especially when compared to Willy's banal Brooklyn neighborhood, crystallize how Willy's obsession with the commercial world of the city has trapped him in an unpleasant reality. Whereas Alaska and the African jungle symbolize Willy's failure, the American West, on the other hand, symbolizes Biff's potential. Biff realizes that he has been content only when working on farms, out in the open. His westward escape from both Willy's delusions and the commercial world of the eastern United States suggests a nineteenth-century pioneer mentality—Biff, unlike Willy, recognizes the importance of the individual.

SYMBOLS

Symbols are objects, characters, figures, and colors used to represent abstract ideas or concepts.

SEEDS

Seeds represent for Willy the opportunity to prove the worth of his labor, both as a salesman and a father. His desperate, nocturnal attempt to grow vegetables signifies his shame about barely being able to put food on the table and having nothing to leave his children when he passes. Willy feels that he has worked hard but fears that he will not be able to help his offspring any more than his own abandoning father helped him. The seeds also symbolize Willy's sense of failure with Biff. Despite the American Dream's formula for success, which Willy considers infallible, Willy's efforts to cultivate and nurture Biff went awry. Realizing that his all-American football star has turned into a lazy bum, Willy takes Biff's failure and lack of ambition as a reflection of his abilities as a father.

DIAMONDS

To Willy, diamonds represent tangible wealth and, hence, both validation of one's labor (and life) and the ability to pass material goods on to one's offspring, two things that Willy desperately craves. Correlatively, diamonds, the discovery of which made Ben a fortune, symbolize Willy's failure as a salesman. Despite Willy's belief in the American Dream, a belief unwavering to the extent that he passed up the opportunity to go with Ben to Alaska, the Dream's promise of financial security has eluded Willy. At the end of the play, Ben encourages Willy to enter the "jungle" finally and retrieve this elusive diamond—that is, to kill himself for insurance money in order to make his life meaningful.

LINDA'S AND THE WOMAN'S STOCKINGS

Willy's strange obsession with the condition of Linda's stockings foreshadows his later flashback to Biff's discovery of him and The Woman in their Boston hotel room. The teenage Biff accuses Willy of giving away Linda's stockings to The Woman. Stockings assume a metaphorical weight as the symbol of betrayal and sexual infidelity. New stockings are important for both Willy's pride in being financially successful and thus able to provide for his family and for Willy's ability to ease his guilt about, and suppress the memory of, his betrayal of Linda and Biff.

THE RUBBER HOSE

The rubber hose is a stage prop that reminds the audience of Willy's desperate attempts at suicide. He has apparently attempted to kill himself by inhaling gas, which is, ironically, the very substance essential to one of the most basic elements with which he must equip his home for his family's health and comfort—heat. Literal death by inhaling gas parallels the metaphorical death that Willy feels in his struggle to afford such a basic necessity.

SYMBOLS

Summary & Analysis

Act I

Opening scene to Willy's first daydream

Summary

The play begins on a Monday evening at the Loman family home in Brooklyn. After some light changes on stage and ambient flute music (the first instance of a motif connected to Willy Loman's faint memory of his father, who was once a flute-maker and salesman), Willy, a sixty-three-year-old traveling salesman, returns home early from a trip, apparently exhausted. His wife, Linda, gets out of bed to greet him. She asks if he had an automobile accident, since he once drove off a bridge into a river. Irritated, he replies that nothing happened. Willy explains that he kept falling into a trance while driving—he reveals later that he almost hit a boy. Linda urges him to ask his employer, Howard Wagner, for a non-traveling job in New York City. Willy's two adult sons, Biff and Happy, are visiting. Before he left that morning, Willy criticized Biff for working at manual labor on farms and horse ranches in the West. The argument that ensued was left unresolved. Willy says that his thirty-four-year-old son is a lazy bum. Shortly thereafter, he declares that Biff is anything but lazy. Willy's habit of contradicting himself becomes quickly apparent in his conversation with Linda.

Willy's loud rambling wakes his sons. They speculate that he had another accident. Linda returns to bed while Willy goes to the kitchen to get something to eat. Happy and Biff reminisce about the good old days when they were young. Although Happy, thirty-two, is younger than Biff, he is more confident and more successful. Biff seems worn, apprehensive, and confused. Happy is worried about Willy's habit of talking to himself. Most of the time, Happy observes, Willy talks to the absent Biff about his disappointment in Biff's unsteadiness. Biff hopped from job to job after high school and is concerned that he has "waste[d] his life." He is disappointed in himself and in the disparity between his life and the notions of value and success with which Willy indoctrinated him as a boy. Happy has a steady job in New York, but the rat race does not satisfy him. He and Biff fantasize briefly about going out west together. However,

Happy still longs to become an important executive. He sleeps with the girlfriends and fiancées of his superiors and often takes bribes in an attempt to climb the corporate ladder from his position as an assistant to the assistant buyer in a department store.

Biff plans to ask Bill Oliver, an old employer, for a loan to buy a ranch. He remembers that Oliver thought highly of him and offered to help him anytime. He wonders if Oliver still thinks that he stole a carton of basketballs while he was working at his store. Happy encourages his brother, commenting that Biff is "well liked"—a sure predictor of success in the Loman household. The boys are disgusted to hear Willy talking to himself downstairs. They try to go to sleep.

ANALYSIS

It is important to note that much of the play's action takes place in Willy's home. In the past, the Brooklyn neighborhood in which the Lomans live was nicely removed from the bustle of New York City. There was space within the neighborhood for expansion and for a garden. When Willy and Linda purchased it, it represented the ultimate expression of Willy's hopes for the future. Now, however, the house is hemmed in by apartment buildings on all sides, and sunlight barely reaches their yard. Their abode has come to represent the reduction of Willy's hopes, even though, ironically, his mortgage payments are almost complete. Just as the house is besieged by apartment buildings, Willy's ego is besieged by doubts and mounting evidence that he will never experience the fame and fortune promised by the American Dream.

Willy's reality profoundly conflicts with his hopes. Throughout his life, he has constructed elaborate fantasies to deny the mounting evidence of his failure to fulfill his desires and expectations. By the time the play opens, Willy suffers from crippling self-delusion. His consciousness is so fractured that he cannot even maintain a consistent fantasy. In one moment, he calls Biff a lazy bum. In the next, he says that Biff is anything but lazy. His later assessment of the family car is similarly contradictory—one moment he calls it a piece of trash, the next "the finest car ever built." Labeling Biff a lazy bum allows Willy to deflect Linda's criticism of his harangue against Biff's lack of material success, ambition, and focus. Denying Biff's laziness enables Willy to hold onto the hope that Biff will someday, in some capacity, fulfill his expectations of him. Willy changes his interpretation of reality according to his psychological needs at the moment. He is likewise able to reimagine decisive moments in his past in his later daydreams. Ironically, he asks Linda angrily why he is "always being contradicted," when it is usually he who contradicts himself from moment to moment.

The opening pages of the play introduce the strangely affected and stilted tone of the dialogue, which transcends the 1950s idiom of nonspecific pet names (an ungendered "pal" or "kid" for adult and child alike) and dated metaphors, vocabulary, and slang. Some critics cite the driving, emphatic, repetitive diction ("Maybe it's your glasses. You never went for your new glasses"; "I'm the New England man. I'm vital in New England") and persistent vexed questioning ("Why do you get American when I like Swiss?" "How can they whip cheese?") as a particularly Jewish-American idiom, but the stylization of the speech serves a much more immediate end than stereotype or bigotry. Miller intended the singsong melodies of his often miserable and conflicted characters to parallel the complex struggle of a family with a skewed version of the American Dream trying to support itself. The dialogue's crooked, blunt lyricism of stuttering diction occasionally rises even to the level of the grotesque and inarticulate, as do the characters themselves. Miller himself claims in his autobiography that the characters in *Death of a Salesman* speak in a stylized manner "to lift the experience into emergency speech of an unabashedly open kind rather than to proceed by the crabbed dramatic hints and pretexts of the 'natural.'"

ACT I (CONTINUED)

Willy's first daydream to the first appearance of The Woman

SUMMARY

Willy is lost in his memories. Suddenly, the memories of his sons' childhood come alive. Young Biff and Happy wash and wax their father's car after he has just returned from a sales trip. Biff informs Willy that he "borrowed" a football from the locker room to practice. Willy laughs knowingly. Happy tries to get his father's attention, but Willy's preference for Biff is obvious. Willy whispers that he will soon open a bigger business than his successful neighbor Uncle Charley because Charley is not as "well liked" as he is. Charley's son, Bernard, arrives to beg Biff to study math with him. Biff is close to failing math, which would prevent him from graduating. Willy orders Biff to study. Biff distracts him by showing him that he printed the insignia of the University of Virginia on his sneakers, impressing Willy. Bernard states that the sneakers do not mean Biff will graduate. After Bernard leaves, Willy asks if Bernard is liked. The boys reply that he is liked but not "well liked." Willy tells them that Bernard may make good grades, but Happy and Biff will be more successful in business because they are "well liked."

Still in his daydream of fifteen years ago, Willy brags to Linda that he made $1200 in sales that week. Linda quickly figures his commission at over $200. Willy then hedges his estimation. Under questioning, he admits that he grossed only $200. The $70 commission is barely adequate to cover the family's expenses. In a rare moment of lucidity and self-criticism, Willy moans that he cannot move ahead because people do not seem to like him. Linda tells him that he is successful enough. Willy complains that he talks and jokes too much. He explains that Charley earns respect because he is a man of few words. His jealousy of his neighbor becomes painfully clear. Willy thinks people laugh at him for being too fat; he once punched a man for joking about his "walrus" physique. As Linda assures him that he is the handsomest man ever, Willy replies that she is his best friend in the world. Just as he tells her that he misses her terribly when he is on the road, The Woman's laughter sounds from the darkness.

<hr />

ANALYSIS

One of the most interesting aspects of *Death of a Salesman* is its fluid treatment of time: past and present flow into one another seamlessly and simultaneously as various stimuli induce in Willy a rambling stream-of-consciousness. It is important to remember that the idyllic past that Willy recalls is one that he reinvents; one should not, therefore, take these seeming flashbacks entirely as truth. The idyllic past functions as an escape from the present reality or a retrospective reconstruction of past events and blunders. Even when he retreats to this idyllic past, however, Willy cannot completely deny his real situation. He retreats into his daydreams not only to escape the present but also to examine the past. He searches for the mistake that he made that frustrated his hopes for fame and fortune and destroyed his relationship with Biff. Willy's treatment of his life as a story to be edited and rewritten enables him to avoid confronting its depressing reality.

It is important to examine the evolution of Willy's relationship with his family, as the solid family is one of the most prominent elements of the American Dream. In the present, Willy's relationship with his family is fraught with tension. In his memories, on the other hand, Willy sees his family as happy and secure. But even Willy's conception of the past is not as idyllic as it seems on the surface, as his split consciousness, the profound rift in his psyche, shows through. No matter how much he wants to remember his past as all-American and blissful, Willy cannot completely erase the evidence to the contrary. He wants to remember Biff as the bright hope for the future. In the midst of his memories, however, we find that Willy does nothing to discourage Biff's compulsive thieving habit. In fact, he subtly encourages it by laughing at Biff's theft of the football.

As an adult, Biff has never held a steady job, and his habitual stealing from employers seems largely to be the reason for this failing. Over the years, Biff and Willy have come to a mutual antagonism. Willy is unable to let go of his commitment to the American Dream, and he places tremendous pressure on Biff to fulfill it for him. Biff feels a deep sense of inadequacy because Willy wants him to pursue a career that conflicts with his natural inclinations and instincts. He would rather work in the open air on a ranch than enter business and make a fortune, and he believes that Willy's natural inclination is the same, like his father's before him.

Willy's relationship with Happy is also less than perfect in Willy's reconstruction of the past, and it is clear that he favors Biff. Happy tries several times to gain Willy's attention and approval but fails. The course of Happy's adult life clearly bears the marks of this favoritism. Happy doesn't express resentment toward Biff; rather, he emulates the behavior of the high-school-aged Biff. In the past, Willy expressed admiration for Biff's success with the girls and his ability to get away with theft. As an adult, Happy competes with more successful men by sleeping with their women—he thus performs a sort of theft and achieves sexual prowess.

Willy's relationship with Linda is even more complex and interesting. In one of his moments of self-doubt, she assures him that he is a good provider and that he is handsome. She also sees through his lie when he tries to inflate his commission from his latest trip. Although she does not buy his pitch to her, she still loves him. His failure to make her believe his fantasy of himself does not lead her to reject him—she does not measure Willy's worth in terms of his professional success. Willy, however, needs more than love, which accepts character flaws, doubts, and insecurity—he seeks desperately to be "well liked." As such, he ignores the opportunity that Linda

presents to him: to view himself more honestly, to acknowledge the reality of his life, and to accept himself for what he is without feeling like a failure. Instead, he tries to play the salesman with her and their sons.

ACT I (CONTINUED)

After The Woman's laughter through Ben's first appearance in Willy's daydream

SUMMARY

The Woman is Willy's mistress and a secretary for one of his buyers. In Willy's daydream, they sit in a hotel room. She tells him that she picked him because he is so funny and sweet. Willy loves the praise. She thanks Willy for giving her stockings and promises to put him right through to the buyers when she sees him next. The Woman fades into the darkness as Willy returns to his conversation with Linda in the present. He notices Linda mending stockings and angrily demands that she throw them out—he is too proud to let his wife wear an old pair (Biff later discovers that Willy has been buying new stockings for The Woman instead of for Linda). Bernard returns to the Loman house to beg Biff to study math. Willy orders him to give Biff the answers. Bernard replies that he cannot do so during a state exam. Bernard insists that Biff return the football. Linda comments that some mothers fear that Biff is "too rough" with their daughters. Willy, enraged by the unglamorous truth of his son's behavior, plunges into a state of distraction and shouts at them to shut up. Bernard leaves the house, and Linda leaves the room, holding back tears.

The memory fades. Willy laments to himself and Happy that he did not go to Alaska with his brother, Ben, who acquired a fortune at the age of twenty-one upon discovering an African diamond mine. Charley, having heard the shouts, visits to check on Willy. They play cards. Charley, concerned about Willy, offers him a job, but Willy is insulted by the offer. He asks Charley if he saw the ceiling he put in his living room, but he becomes surly when Charley expresses interest, insisting that Charley's lack of skill with tools proves his lack of masculinity. Ben appears on the stage in a semi-daydream. He cuts a dignified, utterly confident figure. Willy tells Charley that Ben's wife wrote from Africa to tell them Ben had died. He alternates between conversing with Charley and his dead brother. Willy gets angry when Charley wins a hand, so Charley takes his cards and leaves.

He is disturbed that Willy is so disoriented that he talks to a dead brother as if he were present. Willy immerses himself in the memory of a visit from his brother. Ben and Willy's father abandoned the family when Willy was three or four years old and Ben was seventeen. Ben left home to look for their father in Alaska but never found him. At Willy's request, Ben tells young Biff and Happy about their grandfather. Among an assortment of other jobs, Willy and Ben's father made flutes and sold them as a traveling salesman before following a gold rush to Alaska. Ben proceeds to wrestle the young Biff to the ground in a demonstration of unbridled machismo, wielding his umbrella threateningly over Biff's eye. Willy begs Ben to stay longer, but Ben hurries to catch his train.

ANALYSIS

Just as the product that Willy sells is never specified, so too does The Woman, with whom Willy commits adultery, remain nameless. Miller offers no description of her looks or character because such details are irrelevant; The Woman merely represents Willy's discontent in life. Indeed, she is more a symbol than an actual human being: she regards herself as a means for Willy to get to the buyers more efficiently, and Willy uses her as a tool to feel well liked. Biff sees her as a sign that Willy and his ambitions are not as great as Willy claims.

Willy's compulsive need to be "well liked" contributes to his descent into self-delusion. Whereas Linda loves Willy despite his considerable imperfections, Willy's mistress, on the other hand, merely likes him. She buys his sales pitch, which boosts his ego, but does not care for him deeply the way Linda does. Linda regards Willy's job merely as a source of income; she draws a clear line between Willy as a salesman and Willy as her husband. Willy is unable to do so and thus fails to accept the love that Linda and his sons offer him.

Willy was first abandoned by his father and later by his older brother, Ben. Willy's father was a salesman as well, but he actually produced what he sold and was successful, according to Ben, at least. Ben presents their father as both an independent thinker and a masculine man skilled with his hands. In a sense, Willy's father, not Willy himself, represents the male ideal to Biff, a pioneer spirit and rugged individualist. Unlike his father, Willy does not attain personal satisfaction from the things that he sells because they are not the products of his personal efforts—what he sells is himself, and he is severely damaged and psychically ruptured. His professional persona is the only thing that he has produced himself. In a roundabout manner, Willy seeks approval from his professional contacts by trying to be "well liked"—a coping strategy to deal with his abandonment by the two most important male figures in his life.

Willy's efforts to create the perfect family of the American Dream seem to constitute an attempt to rebuild the pieces of the broken family of his childhood. One can interpret his decision to become a salesman as the manifestation of his desperate desire to be the good father and provider that his own salesman father failed to be. Willy despairs about leaving his sons nothing in the form of a material inheritance, acutely aware that his own father abandoned him and left him with nothing.

Willy's obsession with being well liked seems to be rooted in his reaction to his father's and brother's abandoning of him—he takes their rejection of him as a sign of their not liking him enough. Willy's memory of Ben's visit to his home is saturated with fears of abandonment and a need for approval. When Ben declares that he must leave soon in order to catch his train, Willy desperately tries to find some way to make him stay a little longer. He proudly shows his sons to Ben, practically begging for a word of approval. Additionally, he pleads with Ben to tell Biff and Happy about their grandfather, as he realizes that he has no significant family history to give to his sons as an inheritance; the ability to pass such a chronicle on to one's offspring is an important part of the American Dream that Willy so highly esteems.

ACT I (CONTINUED)

From Ben's departure through the closing scene

SUMMARY

Willy's shouts wake Linda and Biff, who find Willy outside in his slippers. Biff asks Linda how long he has been talking to himself, and Happy joins them outside. Linda explains that Willy's mental unbalance results from his having lost his salary (he now works only on commission). Linda knows that Willy borrows fifty dollars a week from Charley and pretends it is his salary. Linda claims that Biff and Happy are ungrateful. She calls Happy a "philandering bum." Angry and guilt-ridden, Biff offers to stay home and get a job to help with expenses. Linda says that he cannot fight with Willy all the time. She explains that all of his automobile accidents are actually failed suicide attempts. She adds that she found a rubber hose behind the fuse box and a new nipple on the water heater's gas pipe—a sign that Willy attempted to asphyxiate himself. Willy overhears Biff, Happy, and Linda arguing about him. When Biff jokes with his father to snap him out of his trance, Willy misunderstands and thinks that Biff is calling him crazy. They argue, and Willy maintains that he is a "big shot" in the sales world.

Happy mentions that Biff plans to ask Bill Oliver for a business loan. Willy brightens immediately. Happy outlines a publicity campaign to sell sporting goods; the business proposal, which revolves around the brothers using their natural physical abilities to lead publicity displays of sporting events, is thenceforth referred to as the "Florida idea." Everyone loves the idea of Happy and Biff going into business together. Willy begins offering dubious and somewhat unhelpful advice for Biff's loan interview. One moment, he tells Biff not to crack any jokes; the next, he tells him to lighten things up with a couple of funny stories. Linda tries to offer support, but Willy tells her several times to be quiet. He orders Biff not to pick up anything that falls off Oliver's desk because doing so is an office boy's job. Before they fall asleep, Linda again begs Willy to ask his boss for a non-traveling job. Biff removes the rubber hose from behind the fuse box before he retires to bed.

ANALYSIS

One reason for Willy's reluctance to criticize Biff for his youthful thefts and his careless attitude toward his classes seems to be that he fears doing damage to Biff's ego. Thus, he offers endless praise, hoping that Biff will fulfill the promise of that praise in his adulthood. It is also likely that Willy refuses to criticize the young Biff because he fears that, if he does so, Biff will not like him. This disapproval represents the ultimate personal and professional (the two spheres are conflated in Willy's mind) insult and failure. Because Willy's consciousness is split between despair and hope, it is probable that both considerations are behind Willy's decision not to criticize Biff's youthful indiscretions. In any case, his relationship with Biff is fraught, on Willy's side, with the childhood emotional trauma of abandonment and, on Biff's side, with the struggle between fulfilling societal expectations and personal expectations.

The myth of the American Dream has its strongest pull on the individuals who do not enjoy the happiness and prosperity that it promises. Willy pursues the fruits of that dream as a panacea for the disappointments and the hurts of his own youth. He is a true believer in the myth that any "well liked" young man possessing a certain degree of physical faculty and "personal attractiveness" can achieve the Dream if he journeys forth in the world with a can-do attitude of confidence. The men who should have offered him the affirmation that he needed to build a healthy concept of self-worth—his father and Ben—left him. Therefore, Willy tries to measure his self-worth by the standards of an American myth that hardly corresponds to reality, while ignoring the more important foundations of family love, unconditional support, and the freedom of choice inherent to the American Dream. Unfortunately, Willy has a corrupted interpretation of the American Dream that clashes with that set forth by the country's founding fathers; he is preoccupied with the material facets of American success and national identity.

In his obsession with being "well liked," Willy ignores the love that his family can offer him. Linda is far more realistic and grounded than Willy, and she is satisfied with what he can give her. She sees through his facade and still loves and accepts the man behind the facade. She likewise loves her adult sons, and she recognizes their bluster as transparent as well. She knows in her heart that Biff is irresponsible and that Happy is a "philandering bum," but she loves them without always having to like or condone their behavior. The emotional core of the family, Linda demands their full cooperation in dealing with Willy's mental decline. If Willy were content finally to relinquish the gnarled and grotesquely caricatured American tragic myth that he has fed with his fear, insecurity, and profound anxiety and that has possessed his soul, he could be more content. Instead, he continues to chase the fame and fortune that outruns him. He has built his concept of himself not on human relationships that fulfill human needs but on the unrealistic myth of the American hero. That myth has preyed on his all-too-common male weaknesses, until the fantasy that he has constructed about his life becomes intolerable to Biff. Willy's diseased mind is almost ready to explode by the end of Act I. The false hope offered by the "Florida idea" is a placebo, and the empty confidence it instills in Willy makes his final fall all the more crushing.

ACT II

Opening scene through scene in Howard's office

SUMMARY

When Willy awakes the next morning, Biff and Happy have already left, Biff to see Bill Oliver and Happy to mull over the "Florida idea" and go to work. Willy, in high spirits with the prospect of the "Florida idea," mentions that he would like to get some seeds and plant a small garden in the yard. Linda, pleased with her husband's hopeful mood, points out that there is not enough sun. Willy replies that they will have to get a house in the country. Linda reminds Willy to ask his boss, Howard, for a non-traveling job as well as an advance to pay the insurance premium. They have one last payment on both the refrigerator and the house, and they have just finished paying for the car. Linda informs Willy that Biff and Happy want to take him to dinner at Frank's Chop House at six o'clock. As Willy departs, moved and excited by his sons' dinner invitation, he notices a stocking that Linda is mending and, guilt-ridden with the latent memory of his adultery with The Woman, admonishes her to throw the stocking away.

Willy timidly enters Howard's office. Howard is playing with a wire recorder he has just purchased for dictation. He plays the recorded voices of his family: his cloyingly enthusiastic children (a whistling daughter and a son who recites the state capitals in alphabetical order) and his shy wife. As Willy tries to express admiration, Howard repeatedly shushes him. Willy asks for a non-traveling job at $65 a week. Howard replies that there is no opening available. He looks for his lighter. Willy finds it and hands it to him, unconsciously ignoring, in his nervous and pathetically humble distraction, his own advice never to handle or tend to objects in a superior's office, since that is the responsibility of "office boys." Willy keeps lowering his salary request, explaining his financial situation in unusually candid detail, but Howard remains resistant. Howard keeps calling him "kid" and assumes a condescending tone despite his younger age and Willy's reminders that he helped Howard's father name him.

> *I realized that selling was the greatest career a man could want.* (*See* QUOTATIONS, *p. 44*)

Desperate, Willy tries to relate an anecdote about Dave Singleman, an eighty-four-year-old salesman who phoned his buyers and made his sales without ever leaving his hotel room. After he died the noble "death of a salesman" that eludes Willy, hundreds of salesmen and buyers attended his funeral. Willy reveals that his acquaintance with this venerable paragon of salesmanship convinced him to become a salesman himself rather than join his brother, Ben, on his newly purchased plot of timberland in Alaska. Singleman's dignified success and graceful, respected position as an older man deluded Willy into believing that "selling was the greatest career a man could want" because of its limitless potential and its honorable nature. Willy laments the loss of friendship and personality in the business, and he complains that no one knows him anymore. An uninterested Howard leaves the office to attend to other people, and he returns when Willy begins shouting frantically after accidentally switching on the wire recorder. Eventually, Willy becomes so distraught that Howard informs him that he does not want Willy to represent his company anymore. Howard essentially fires Willy, with the vague implication of reemployment after a period of "rest." He suggests that Willy turn to his sons (who he understandably assumes are successful given Willy's loud bragging) for financial support, but Willy is horrified at the thought of depending on his children and reversing the expected familial roles. He is far too proud to admit defeat, and Howard must insist repeatedly on the cessation of Willy's employment before it sinks in.

ANALYSIS

Biff's decision to seek a business loan raises Willy's spirits, and the way in which Willy expresses his optimism is quite revealing. The first thing Willy thinks about is planting a garden in his yard; he then muses to Linda that they should buy a house in the country, so that he could build guesthouses for Biff and Happy when they have families of their own. These hopeful plans seem to illustrate how ill-suited Willy is to his profession, as it stifles his natural inclinations. Indeed, the competitive, hyper-capitalist world of sales seems no more appropriate for Willy than for Biff. Willy seems happiest when he dreams of building things with his own hands, and when his instincts in this direction surface, he seems whole again, able to see a glimmer of truth in himself and his abilities.

Willy's wistful fantasy of living in the forests of Alaska strengthens the implication that he chose the wrong profession. He does not seem to like living in an urban setting. However, his fascination with the frontier is also intimately connected to his obsession with the American Dream. In nineteenth-century America, the concept of the intrepid explorer entering the unknown, uncharted wilderness and striking gold was deeply imbedded in the national consciousness. With the postwar surge of consumerism in America, this "wilderness" became the bustling market of consumer goods, and the capitalist replaced the pioneer as the American hero. These new intrepid explorers plunged into the jungle of business transactions in order to find a niche to exploit. Ben, whose success involved a literal jungle in Africa, represents one version of the frontier narrative. Dave Singleman represents another. Willy chose to follow Singleman's path, convinced that it was the modern version and future of the American Dream of success through hard work.

While Willy's dissatisfaction with his life seems due in part to choosing a profession that conflicts with his interests, it seems also due in part to comparing all aspects, professional and private alike, of his own life to those of a mythic standard. He fails to realize that Ben's wealth is the result of a blind stroke of luck rather than a long-deserved reward for hard work and personal merit. Similarly, Willy misses the tragic aspect of Singleman's story of success—that Singleman was still working at the age of eighty-four and died on the job. Mourning for him was limited to the sphere of salesmen and train passengers who happened to be there at his death—the ephemeral world of transience, travel, and money, as opposed to the meaningful realm of loved ones.

Willy's humiliating interview with Howard sheds some light on his advice for Biff's interview with Oliver. This advice clearly has its roots in Willy's relationship with his boss. Despite being much younger than Willy, Howard patronizes Willy by repeatedly calling him "kid." Willy proves entirely subservient to Howard, as evidenced by the fact that he picks up Howard's lighter and hands it to him, unable to follow his own advice about such office boy jobs.

Willy's repeated reminders to Howard that he helped his father name Howard illustrate his psychological reliance on outmoded and insubstantial concepts of chivalry and nobility. Like his emphasis on being "well liked," Willy's harping upon the honor of bestowing Howard's name—one can draw a parallel between this naming and the sanctity and dignity of medieval concepts of christening and the dubbing of knights—is anachronistically incompatible with the reality of the modern business world.

Willy seems to transfer his familial anxieties to his professional life. His brother and father did not like him enough to stay, so he endeavors to be "well liked" in his profession. He heard the story of Dave Singleman's success and exaggerated it to heroic, mythical proportions. Hundreds of people attended Singleman's funeral— obviously, he was a man who was "well liked." Dave Singleman's story hooked Willy as the key to emotional and psychological fulfillment. However, the inappropriateness of Willy's ideals reveals itself in his lament about the loss of friendship and camaraderie in his profession. Willy fantasizes about such things, and he used to tell his sons about all of his friends in various cities; as Willy's hard experience evidences, however, such camaraderie belongs only to the realm of his delusion.

ACT II (CONTINUED)

Willy's daydream involving Ben through Willy's conversation with Charley in his office

SUMMARY

After Howard leaves, Willy immerses himself in memories of a visit from Ben. Ben asks Willy to go to Alaska and manage a tract of timberland he has purchased. Linda, slightly afraid of Ben, says that Willy already has a nice job. Ben departs as Willy tries desperately to gain a word of approval from him, comparing the intangible success of the honorable Dave Singleman to the concrete possibilities of timber. Bernard arrives to accompany the Lomans to the big football game at Ebbets Field. He begs Biff to allow him to carry his helmet. Happy snaps and insists on carrying it. Biff generously allows Bernard to carry his shoulder pads. Charley ambles over to tease Willy a little about the immature importance he is placing on the football game, and Willy grows furious.

In the present, the grown-up Bernard is sitting in his father's reception room when his father's secretary, Jenny, enters to beg him to deal with Willy. Outside, Willy, still immersed in his memory, argues with an invisible Charley from the past about Biff's football game. Bernard converses with Willy and mentions that he has a case to argue in Washington, D.C. Willy replies that Biff is working on a very big deal in town. Willy breaks down and asks Bernard why Biff's life seemed to end after his big football game. Bernard mentions that Biff failed math but was determined to go to summer school and pass. He adds that Biff went to see Willy in Boston, but after he came back, he burned his sneakers with the University of Virginia's insignia. Attempting a candid conversation with the wounded Willy, Bernard asks him what happened in Boston that changed Biff's intentions and drained his motivation. Willy becomes angry and resentful and demands to know if Bernard blames him for Biff's failure. Charley exits his office to say goodbye to Bernard. He mentions that Bernard is arguing a case before the Supreme Court. Willy, simultaneously jealous and proud of Bernard, is astounded that Bernard did not mention it.

In his office, Charley counts out fifty dollars. With difficulty, Willy asks for over a hundred this time to pay his insurance fees. After a moment, Charley states that he has offered Willy a non-traveling job with a weekly salary of fifty dollars and scolds Willy for insulting him. Willy refuses the job again, insisting that he already has one, despite Charley's reminder that Willy earns no money at his job. Broken, he admits that Howard fired him. Outraged and incredulous, he again mentions that he chose Howard's name when he was born. Charley replies that Willy cannot sell that sort of thing. Willy retorts that he has always thought the key to success was being well liked. Exasperated, Charley asks who liked J. P. Morgan. He angrily gives Willy the money for his insurance. Willy shuffles out of the office in tears.

ANALYSIS

Willy's conversation with Bernard revives Willy's attempt to understand why Biff never made a material success of his life despite his bright and promising youth. He wants to understand why the "well liked" teenage football player became an insecure man unable to hold a steady job. He assumes there is some secret to success that is not readily apparent. If he were not wearing the rose-colored glasses of the myth of the American Dream, he would see that Charley and his son are successful because of lifelong hard work and not because of the illusions of social popularity and physical appearances.

Biff's failure in math is symbolic of his failure to live up to his father's calculated plan for him. Willy believes so blindly in his interpretation of the American Dream that he has constructed a veritable formula by which he expects Biff to achieve success. The unshakeable strength of Willy's belief in this blueprint for success is evidenced later when he attempts to plant the vegetable seeds. Reading the instructions on the seed packets, Willy mutters, as he measures out the garden plot, "carrots . . . quarter-inch apart. Rows . . . one-foot rows." He has applied the same regimented approach to the cultivation of his sons. Biff struggles with this formula in the same way that he struggles with the formulas in his textbook.

Charley tries to bring Willy down to earth by explaining that Willy's fantasies about the way the business world functions conflict with the reality of a consumer economy. Charley refuses to relate to Willy through blustering fantasy; instead, he makes a point of being frank. He states that the bottom line of business is selling and buying, not being liked. Ironically, Charley is the only person to offer Willy a business opportunity on the strength of a personal bond; Howard, in contrast, fires Willy *despite* the strong friendship that Willy shared with Howard's father. However, the relationship between Willy and Charley is shaped by an ongoing competition between their respective families, at least from Willy's point of view. Willy's rejection of Charley's job offer stems partly from jealousy of Charley's success. Additionally, Willy knows that Charley does not like him much—his offer of a job thus fails to conform to Willy's idealistic notions about business relationships. Willy chooses to reject a well-paying, secure job rather than let go of the myth of the American business world and its ever receding possibilities for success and redemption.

For Willy, the American Dream has become a kind of Holy Grail—his childish longing for acceptance and material proof of success in an attempt to align his life with a mythic standard has assumed the dimensions of a religious crusade. He places his faith in the elusive American Dream because he seeks salvation, and he blindly expects to achieve material, emotional, and even spiritual satisfaction through "personal attractiveness" and being "well liked." Willy forces Biff and Happy into the framework of this mythic quest for secular salvation—he even calls them "Adonis" and "Hercules," envisioning them as legendary figures whose greatness has destined them to succeed in according to the American Dream.

Act II (continued)

The scene in Frank's Chop House

Summary

Happy banters with the waiter, Stanley. Happy is flirting with a pretty girl named Miss Forsythe when Biff arrives to join him. After she responds to his pick-up line by claiming that she is, in fact, a cover girl, Happy tells her that he is a successful champagne salesman and that Biff is a famous football player. Judging from Happy's repeated comments on her moral character and his description of her as "on call," Miss Forsythe is probably a prostitute. Happy invites her to join them. She exits to make a phone call to cancel her previous plans and to invite a girlfriend to join them. Biff explains to Happy that he waited six hours to see Oliver, only to have Oliver not even remember him. Biff asks where he got the idea that he was a salesman for Oliver. He had actually been only a lowly shipping clerk, but somehow Willy's exaggerations and lies had transformed him into a salesman in the Loman family's collective memory. After Oliver and the secretary left, Biff recounts, he ran into Oliver's office and stole his fountain pen.

Happy advises Biff to tell Willy that Oliver is thinking over his business proposition, claiming that eventually the whole situation will fade away from their father's memory. When Willy arrives, he reveals that he has been fired and states that he wants some good news to tell Linda. Despite this pressure, Biff attempts to tell the truth. Disoriented, Willy shouts that Biff cannot blame everything on him because Biff is the one who failed math after all. Confused at his father's crazed emphasis on his high school math failure, Biff steels himself to forge ahead with the truth, but the situation reaches crisis proportions when Willy absolutely refuses to listen to Biff's story. In a frenzy as the perilous truth closes in on him, Willy enters a semi-daydream state, reliving Biff's discovery of him and The Woman in their Boston hotel room. A desperate Biff backs down and begins to lie to assuage his frantic father. Miss Forsythe returns with her friend, Letta. Willy, insulted at Biff's "spite," furiously lashes out at his son's attempts to explain himself and the impossibility of returning to Oliver. Willy wanders into the restroom, talking to himself, and an embarrassed Happy informs the women that he is not, in fact, their father. Biff angrily tells Happy to help Willy, accusing him of not caring about their father. He hurries out of the restaurant in a vortex of guilt and anguish. Happy frantically asks Stanley for the bill; when the waiter doesn't respond immediately, Happy rushes after Biff, pushing Miss Forsythe and Letta along in front of him and leaving Willy babbling alone in the restroom.

ANALYSIS

Willy's encounters with Howard, Bernard, and Charley constitute serious blows to the fantasy through which he views his life; his constructed reality is falling apart. Biff has also experienced a moment of truth, but he regards his epiphany as a liberating experience from a lifetime of stifling and distorting lies. He wishes to leave behind the facade of the Loman family tradition so that he and his father can begin to relate to one another honestly. Willy, on the other hand, wants his sons to aid him in rebuilding the elaborate fantasies that deny his reality as a defeated man. Willy drives Biff to produce a falsely positive report of his interview with Oliver, and Happy is all too willing to comply. When Biff fails to produce the expected glowing report, Happy, who has not had the same revelation as Biff, chimes in with false information about the interview.

Willy's greatest fear is realized during his ill-fated dinner with Biff and Happy. In his moment of weakness and defeat, he asks for their help in rebuilding his shattered concept of his life; he is not very likable, and he is well aware of it. Biff and Happy's neglect of him fits into a pattern of abandonment. Like Willy's father, then Ben, then Howard, Biff and Happy erode Willy's fantasy world. The scene in Frank's Chop House is pivotal to Willy's unraveling and to Biff's disillusionment. Biff's epiphany in Oliver's office regarding Willy's exaggeration of Biff's position at Oliver's store puts him on a quest to break through the thick cloud of lies surrounding his father at any cost. Just as Willy refuses to hear what he doesn't want to accept, Biff refuses to subject himself further to his father's delusions.

Willy's pseudo-religious quest for success is founded on a complex, multilayered delusion, and Biff believes that for his father to die well (in the medieval, Christian sense of the word—much of the play smacks of the anachronistic absurdity of the medieval values of chivalry and blind faith), he must break through the heavy sediment of lies to the truth of his personal degradation. Both Willy and Biff are conscious of the disparity between Dave Singleman's mythic "death of a salesman" and the pathetic nature of Willy's impending death. Willy clings to the hope that the "death of a salesman" is necessarily noble by the very nature of the profession, whereas Biff understands that behind the veneer of the American Dream's empty promises lies a devastatingly lonely death diametrically opposed to the one that Singleman represents and that the Dream itself posits. Happy and Linda wish to allow Willy to die covered by the diminishing comfort of his delusions, but Biff feels a moral responsibility to try to reveal the truth.

ACT II (CONTINUED)

Boston hotel room daydream through Willy's departure from Frank's Chop House

SUMMARY

Upon his sons' departure from Frank's Chop House, Willy is immersed in the memory of the teenage Biff's visit to see him in Boston. In his daydream it is night and he is in a hotel room with his mistress, while in the present he is presumably still in the restroom of Frank's Chop House. Biff is outside knocking on the hotel room door, after telephoning the room repeatedly with no result. The Woman, who is dressing, pesters Willy to answer the door. She flirtatiously describes how he has "ruined" her, and she offers to send him straight through to the buyers whom she represents the next time he visits Boston on business. Willy, who is clearly nervous about his surprise visitor, finally consents to her appeals to answer the door. He orders her to stay in the bathroom and be quiet, believing it may be a nosy hotel clerk investigating their affair.

Willy answers the door, and Biff reports that he failed math. He asks Willy to persuade the teacher, Mr. Birnbaum, to pass him. Willy tries to get Biff out of the room quickly with promises of a malted drink and a rapid trip home to talk to the math teacher. When Biff mockingly imitates his teacher's lisp, The Woman laughs from the bathroom. She exits the bathroom, wearing only a negligee, and Willy pushes her out into the hallway. He tries to pass her off as a buyer staying in the room next door who needed to shower in Willy's bathroom because her room was being painted. Biff sits on his suitcase, crying silently, not buying his father's lies. Willy promises to talk to the math teacher, but Biff tells him to forget it because no one will listen to a phony liar. He resolves not to make up the math test and not to attend college, effectively negating his contracted role in Willy's inflated version of the American Dream. He deals the most serious blow by accusing Willy of giving Linda's stockings away to his mistress. Biff leaves, with Willy kneeling and yelling after him.

Stanley pulls Willy out of his daydream. Willy is on his knees in the restaurant ordering the teenage Biff to come back. Stanley explains his sons' absence, and Willy attempts to tip him, but Stanley stealthily slips the dollar bill back into Willy's coat as he turns. Willy asks him to direct him to a seed store, and he rushes out, frantically explaining that he must plant immediately, as he does not "have a thing in the ground."

> *Nothing's planted. I don't have a thing in the ground.*
>
> *(See* QUOTATIONS, *p. 47)*

ANALYSIS

Willy settles on Biff's discovery of his adultery as the reason for Biff's failure to fulfill Willy's ambitions for him. Before he discovers the affair, Biff believes in Willy's meticulously constructed persona. Afterward, he calls Willy out as a "phony little fake." He sees beneath Willy's facade and rejects the man behind it; to be exposed in this way as a charlatan is the salesman's worst nightmare. Assuming a characteristically simplistic cause-and-effect relationship, Willy decides that Biff's failure to succeed is a direct result of the disillusionment that he experiences as a result of Willy's infidelity. Despising Willy for his affair, Biff must also have come to despise Willy's ambitions for him.

In this reckoning, Willy again conflates the personal with the professional. His understanding of the American Dream as constituting professional success and material gain precludes the idea that one can derive happiness without these things. Ironically, in Willy's daydream this desired tangible proof of success is acquired by means of the immaterial and ephemeral concepts of "personal attractiveness" and being "well liked." Willy believes that Biff, no longer able to respect him as a father or a person, automatically gave up all hopes for achieving the American Dream, since he could not separate Willy's expectations of him from his damaged emotional state. In a sense, Willy is right this time—Biff's knowledge of Willy's adultery tarnishes the package deal of the total Dream, and Biff rejects the flawed product that Willy is so desperately trying to sell him.

Willy's earlier preoccupation with the state of Linda's stockings and her mending them foreshadows the exposure and fall that the Boston incident represents. Until the climactic scene in the restaurant, when Biff first attempts to dispel the myths and lies sinking the Loman household, the only subconscious trace of Willy's adultery is his insistence that Linda throw her old stockings out. The stockings' power as a symbol of his betrayal overcomes Willy when Biff's assault on his increasingly delicate shield of lies forces him to confront his guilt about his affair with The Woman. When Biff, the incarnation of Willy's ambition, rejects the delusion that Willy offers, Willy's faith in the American Dream, which he vested in his son, begins to dissolve as well.

Willy's delirious interest in a seed shop reveals his insecurity about his legacy. Poor and now unemployed, Willy has no means to pass anything on to his sons. Indeed, he has just given Stanley a dollar in a feeble attempt to prove to himself, by being able to give, that he does indeed possess *something*. The act of giving also requires *someone* to whom to give, and Stanley becomes, momentarily, a surrogate son to Willy, since Biff and Happy have abandoned him. Similarly, in desperately seeking to grow vegetables, Willy desires tangible proof of the value of his labor, and hence, life. Additionally, the successful growth of vegetables would redeem Willy's failure to cultivate Biff properly. In declaring "Nothing's planted. I don't have a thing in the ground," Willy acknowledges that Biff has broken free from the roots of the long-standing Loman delusion. Finally, Willy's use of gardening as a metaphor for success and failure indicates that he subconsciously acknowledges that, given his natural inclinations toward working with his hands and creating, going into sales was a poor career choice.

Act II (continued)

The boys' confrontation with Linda, Biff's final confrontation with Willy, and Willy's decision to take a late-night drive

Summary

Biff and Happy return home later that night with a bouquet of roses for Linda. She knocks the roses to the ground and shouts at them to pack and never come back. Happy claims that Willy had a great time at dinner. Linda calls her sons a variety of names and accuses them of abandoning their sick father in a restaurant bathroom. Happy, incredulous and defensive, denies everything, but Biff accepts the judgment and wholeheartedly endorses his own degradation and status as "scum of the earth." After searching the house for Willy, Biff hears him outside, and Linda explains that he is maniacally planting a garden regardless of the darkness. Outside, Willy discusses a guaranteed $20,000 proposition with Ben. Ben warns that the insurance company might not honor the policy. Willy retorts that since he has always paid the premium, the company cannot refuse. He says that Biff will realize how important he is once he sees the number of people who attend his funeral. Ben warns that

Biff will call him a coward and hate him. Willy is, of course, contemplating suicide, which would allow his family to cash in on his life insurance policy.

Why am I trying to become what I don't want to be ...
(See QUOTATIONS, *p. 45)*

Biff tells Willy that he is leaving for good and that he will not keep in touch. Biff wants Willy to forget him. Willy curses his son and declares that Biff is throwing his life away and blaming his failures on him out of spite. Biff confronts Willy with the rubber hose. Biff states that he has stolen himself out of every job since high school and that during the three-month period when he was completely out of touch with his family he was, in fact, in prison for stealing a suit. He reproaches Willy for having filled him with so much hot air about how important he, Biff, was that he was unable to take orders from anyone. Further, he accuses the family of never telling the truth "for ten minutes in this house." He exposes Happy's exaggeration of his position—Happy is not the assistant buyer, as he claims, but rather one of two assistants to the assistant buyer—and he says that he does not want to do anything but work in the open air. Biff is determined to know who he is and for his father to know likewise who *he* is. He urges Willy to accept their own commonness—they are both "a dime a dozen," not destined for leadership or worthy of prizes. Crying and exhausted, Biff trudges upstairs to bed. Suddenly happy, Willy mutters that Biff must like him because he cried, and his own delusions of his son's success are restored in light of this meager proof. Linda and Happy tell him that Biff has always loved him, and even Happy seems genuinely moved by the encounter. Everyone retires to bed, except Willy. He urges Linda to sleep and promises that he will join her soon. Willy converses with Ben, predicting that Biff will go far with $20,000 in his pocket. Suddenly, Willy realizes he is alone; Ben has disappeared. Linda calls from upstairs for him to come to bed, but he does not. Happy and Biff listen. They hear the car start and speed away.

ANALYSIS

Willy's final confrontation with Biff exposes the essential gridlock of their relationship. Biff wants Willy to forget him as a useless bum. Once Willy finally lets go of him, Biff can be free to be himself and lead his life without having to carry the weight of his father's dreams. But Willy cannot let go of the myth around which he has built his life. He has no hopes of achieving the American Dream himself, so he has transferred his hopes to Biff. Fulfilling Biff's request would involve discarding his dreams and ambitions forever and admitting that he has long believed in the American Dream for naught. Each man is struggling with the other in a desperate battle for his own identity.

During the confrontation, Biff makes no attempt to blame anyone for the course that his life has taken. He doesn't even mention the affair with The Woman, which Willy imagines as the sole reason for his son's lack of material success. After so many years, Biff doesn't consider his disillusionment a function of either Willy's adultery or the inherent foolishness of Willy's ambitions. Ironically, Biff blames Willy's fantastic success in selling him on the American Dream of easy success as the reason for his failure to hold a steady job. Biff's faith in Willy's dreams is the real reason that he could not advance in the business world. He could not start from the bottom and work his way up because he believed that success would magically descend upon him at any moment, regardless of his own efforts or ambitions.

Willy's happy reaction to Biff's frustrated tears demonstrates that Willy has again missed an opportunity to take refuge in the love of his family. He responds to Biff's tears as material evidence that Biff "likes" him. Linda corrects him with the words "loves you." Willy's failure to recognize the anguished love offered to him by his family is crucial to the climax of his tortured day. Because Willy has long conflated successful salesmanship with being well liked, one can even argue that Willy's imagining that Biff likes him boosts his confidence in his ability to sell and thus perversely enables his final sale—his life.

In Willy's mind, his imminent suicide takes on epic proportions. Not only does it validate his salesmanship, as argued above, but it also renders him a martyr, since he believes that the insurance money from his sacrifice will allow Biff to fulfill the American Dream. Additionally, Ben's final mantra of "The jungle is dark, but full of diamonds" turns Willy's suicide into a metaphorical moral struggle. Suicide, for Willy, constitutes both a final ambition to realize the Dream and the ultimate selfless act of giving to his sons. According to Ben, the noble death that Willy seeks is "not like an appointment at all" but like a "diamond . . . rough and hard to the touch." In the absence of any true self-knowledge, Willy is able, at least, to achieve a tangible result with his suicide. In this way, Willy does experience a sort of revelation: he understands that the product he sells is himself and that his final sale is his own life. Through the imaginary advice of Ben, Willy ultimately believes his earlier assertion to Charley that "after all the highways, and the trains, and the appointments, and the years, you end up worth more dead than alive."

In an analysis of Willy's obsession with the American Dream as a religious crusade, his suicide represents the ultimate apotheosis into the Dream itself, the final expiation for the sins of conflated professional and personal failure. A kind of perverse, American working-class Christ-figure, Willy dies not only for his own sins but also for the sins of his sons, who have failed to achieve their potential within the American Dream.

REQUIEM

SUMMARY

> *He's a man way out there in the blue . . . A salesman is got to dream, boy.*
>
> (See QUOTATIONS, p. 48)

To Linda's considerable chagrin and bewilderment, Willy's family, Charley, and Bernard are the only mourners who attend Willy's funeral. She wonders where all his supposed business friends are and how he could have killed himself when they were so close to paying off all of their bills. Biff recalls that Willy seemed happier working on the house than he did as a salesman. He states that Willy had all the wrong dreams and that he didn't know who he was in the way that Biff now knows who he is. Charley replies that a salesman has to dream or he is lost, and he explains the salesman's undaunted optimism in the face of certain defeat as a function of his irrepressible dreams of selling himself. Happy becomes increasingly angry at Biff's observations. He resolves to stay in the city and carry out his father's dream by becoming a top businessman, convinced he can still "beat this racket." Linda requests some privacy. She reports to Willy that she made the last payment on the house. She apologizes for her inability to cry, since it seems as if Willy is just "on another trip." She begins to sob, repeating, "We're free. . . ." Biff helps her up and all exit. The flute music is heard and the high-rise apartments surrounding the Loman house come into focus.

ANALYSIS

Charley's speech about the nature of the salesman's dreams is one of the most memorable passages in the play. His words serve as a kind of respectful eulogy that removes blame from Willy as an individual by explaining the grueling expectations and absurd demands of his profession. The odd, anachronistic, spiritual formality of his remarks ("Nobody dast blame this man") echo the religious quality of Willy's quest to sell himself. One can argue that, to a certain extent, Willy Loman is the postwar American equivalent of the medieval crusader, battling desperately for the survival of his own besieged faith.

Charley solemnly observes that a salesman's life is a constant upward struggle to sell himself—he supports his dreams on the ephemeral power of his own image, on "a smile and a shoeshine." He suggests that the salesman's condition is an aggravated enlargement of a discreet facet of the general human condition. Just as Willy is blind to the totality of the American Dream, concentrating on the aspects related to material success, so is the salesman, in general, lacking, blinded to the total human experience by his conflation of the professional and the personal. Like Charley says, "No man only needs a little salary"—no man can sustain himself on money and materiality without an emotional or spiritual life to provide meaning.

When the salesman's advertising self-image fails to inspire smiles from customers, he is "finished" psychologically, emotionally, and spiritually. According to Charley, "a salesman is got to dream." The curious and lyrical slang substitution of "is" for "has" indicates a destined necessity for the salesman—not only must the salesman follow the imperative of his dreams during his life, but Miller suggests that he is literally begotten with the sole purpose of dreaming.

In many ways, Willy has done everything that the myth of the American Dream outlines as the key path to success. He acquired a home and the range of modern appliances. He raised a family and journeyed forth into the business world full of hope and ambition. Nevertheless, Willy has failed to receive the fruits that the American Dream promises. His primary problem is that he continues to believe in the myth rather than restructuring his conception of his life and his identity to meet more realistic standards. The values that the myth espouses are not designed to assuage human insecurities and doubts; rather, the myth unrealistically ignores the existence of such weaknesses. Willy bought the sales pitch that America uses to advertise itself, and the price of his faith is death.

Linda's initial feeling that Willy is just "on another trip" suggests that Willy's hope for Biff to succeed with the insurance money will not be fulfilled. To an extent, Linda's comparison debases Willy's death, stripping it of any possibility of the dignity that Willy imagined. It seems inevitable that the trip toward meaningful death that Willy now takes will end just as fruitlessly as the trip from which he has just returned as the play opens. Indeed, the recurrence of the haunting flute music, symbolic of Willy's futile pursuit of the American Dream, and the final visual imprint of the overwhelming apartment buildings reinforce the fact that Willy dies as deluded as he lived.

IMPORTANT QUOTATIONS EXPLAINED

1. And when I saw that, I realized that selling was the greatest
   career a man could want. 'Cause what could be more
   satisfying than to be able to go, at the age of eighty-four,
   into twenty or thirty different cities, and pick up a phone,
   and be remembered and loved and helped by so many
   different people?

Willy poses this question to Howard Wagner in Act II, in Howard's
office. He is discussing how he decided to become a salesman after
meeting Dave Singleman, the mythic salesman who died the noble
"death of a salesman" that Willy himself covets. His admiration of
Singleman's prolonged success illustrates his obsession with being
well liked. He fathoms having people "remember" and "love" him
as the ultimate satisfaction, because such warmth from business
contacts would validate him in a way that his family's love does not.
In so highly esteeming Singleman and deeming his on-the-job death
as dignified, respectable, and graceful, Willy fails to see the human
side of Singleman, much as he fails to see his own human side. He
envisions Singleman as a happy man but ignores the fact that Singleman was still working at age eighty-four and might likely have experienced the same financial difficulties and consequent pressures
and misery as Willy.

2. I saw the things that I love in this world. The work and the food and the time to sit and smoke. And I looked at the pen and I thought, what the hell am I grabbing this for? Why am I trying to become what I don't want to be . . . when all I want is out there, waiting for me the minute I say I know who I am.

Biff's explanation to his father during the climax of their final confrontation in Act II helps him articulate the revelation of his true identity, even though Willy cannot possibly understand. Biff is confident and somewhat comfortable with the knowledge that he is "a dime a dozen," as this escape from his father's delusions allows him to follow his instincts and align his life with his own dreams. Whereas Willy cannot comprehend any notion of individual identity outside of the confines of the material success and "well liked"-ness promised by the American Dream, Biff realizes that he can be happy only *outside* these confines. Though his attempt to cure Willy's delusions fails, Biff frees himself from Willy's expectations for him. He sees the stupidity of stealing the pen and renounces the commercial world, content to enjoy the simple necessities of life.

3. A diamond is hard and rough to the touch.

Ben's final mantra of "The jungle is dark, but full of diamonds" in Act II turns Willy's suicide into a moral struggle and a matter of commerce. His final act, according to Ben, is "not like an appointment at all" but like a "diamond . . . rough and hard to the touch." As opposed to the fruitless, emotionally ruinous meetings that Willy has had with Howard Wagner and Charley, his death, Ben suggests, will actually yield something concrete for Willy and his family. Willy latches onto this appealing idea, relieved to be able finally to prove himself a success in business. Additionally, he is certain that with the $20,000 from his life insurance policy, Biff will at last fulfill the expectations that he, Willy, has long held for him. The diamond stands as a tangible reminder of the material success that Willy's salesman job could not offer him and the missed opportunity of material success with Ben. In selling himself for the metaphorical diamond of $20,000, Willy bears out his earlier assertion to Charley that "after all the highways, and the trains, and the appointments, and the years, you end up worth more dead than alive."

4.   Nothing's planted. I don't have a thing in the ground.

After the climax in Frank's Chop House, in Act II, Willy, talking to Stanley, suddenly fixates on buying seeds to plant a garden in his diminutive, dark backyard because he does not have "a thing in the ground." The garden functions as a last-ditch substitute for Willy's failed career and Biff's dissipated ambition. Willy realizes, at least metaphorically, that he has no tangible proof of his life's work. While he is planting the seeds and conversing with Ben, he worries that "a man can't go out the way he came in," that he has to "add up to something." His preoccupation with material evidence of success belies his very profession, which necessitates the ability to sell one's own, intangible image. The seeds symbolize Willy's failure in other ways as well. The fact that Willy uses gardening as a metaphor for success and failure indicates that he subconsciously acknowledges that his chosen profession is a poor choice, given his natural inclinations. Though his figurative roots are in sales (Ben claims that their father was a successful salesman), Willy never blossomed into the Dave Singleman figure that he idolizes.

5.   He's a man way out there in the blue, riding on a smile and
     a shoeshine . . . A salesman is got to dream, boy.

Charley's speech in the requiem about the nature of the salesman's
dreams eulogizes Willy as a victim of his difficult profession. His
poetic assessment of sales defends Willy's death, attributing to
Willy's work the sort of mythic quality that Willy himself always
envisioned about it. Charley likens the salesman to a heroic, coura-
geous sailor, "out there in the blue," with nothing to guide him and
powerful forces against which to contend. Charley also points out
the great disparity between the enormity of the salesman's task and
the piddling tools with which he is equipped: Willy had only the insubstantial smile on his face and shine of his shoe with which to sell
himself. Failure faded Willy's smile and smudged his shoe, which
made it even more difficult to sell himself. Lacking confidence in his
image and thus "finished" psychologically, Willy still had to go out
and give it his best, because "a salesman is got to dream." Charley's
sympathy reveals itself in this remark—he understands that Willy
didn't simply feel compelled to sell; rather, Willy failed even to recognize that he had any choice in life.

KEY FACTS

FULL TITLE

Death of a Salesman: Certain Private Conversations in Two Acts and a Requiem

AUTHOR

Arthur Miller

TYPE OF WORK

Play

GENRE

Tragedy, social commentary, family drama

LANGUAGE

English (with emphasis on middle-class American lingo)

TIME AND PLACE WRITTEN

Six weeks in 1948, in a shed in Connecticut

DATE OF FIRST PUBLICATION

1949

ORIGINAL PUBLISHER

The Viking Press

CLIMAX

The scene in Frank's Chop House and Biff's final confrontation with Willy at home

PROTAGONISTS

Willy Loman, Biff Loman

ANTAGONISTS

Biff Loman, Willy Loman, the American Dream

SETTING (TIME)

"Today," that is, the present; either the late 1940s or the time period in which the play is being produced, with "daydreams" into Willy's past; all of the action takes place during a twenty-four-hour period between Monday night and Tuesday night, except the "Requiem," which takes place, presumably, a few days after Willy's funeral

SETTING (PLACE)

According to the stage directions, "Willy Loman's house and yard [in Brooklyn] and . . . various places he visits in . . . New York and Boston"

FALLING ACTION

The "Requiem" section, although the play is not really structured as a classical drama

TENSE

Present

FORESHADOWING

Willy's flute theme foreshadows the revelation of his father's occupation and abandonment; Willy's preoccupation with Linda's stockings foreshadows his affair with The Woman; Willy's automobile accident before the start of Act I foreshadows his suicide at the end of Act II

TONE

The tone of Miller's stage directions and dialogue ranges from sincere to parodying, but, in general, the treatment is tender, though at times brutally honest, toward Willy's plight

THEMES

The American Dream; abandonment; betrayal

MOTIFS

Mythic figures; the American West; Alaska; the African jungle

SYMBOLS

Seeds; diamonds; Linda's and The Woman's stockings; the rubber hose

KEY FACTS

STUDY QUESTIONS

1. *How does Willy's home function as a metaphor for his ambitions?*

When Willy and Linda purchased their home, the neighborhood was quieter than they now find it. The house was surrounded by space and sunlight. Willy was a young man with ambitious hopes for the future, and his house represented a space in which he could expand his dreams. In the present, the house is hemmed in on all sides by apartment units. Willy is a much older man, and his chances of achieving his dreams are much slimmer. His home now represents the reduction of his hopes. There is less room to expand, and the sunlight does not even reach into his yard. In the past, the house was the site of hopeful departure and triumphant return. Willy would set out each week to make a load of money. When he returned, his worshipful sons greeted him, and he whispered into their eager ears his hopes to open his own business. Now, the house is the site of Willy's frustrated ambitions. When the play opens, Willy returns to his home a defeated man, unable to complete his latest business trip, and with his argument with Biff left unresolved.

2. *What role does the fear of abandonment play in Willy's life?*

Willy's obsession with making his family conform to the ideals of the American Dream seems rooted in the childhood emotional trauma of his abandonment by his father. Since his father left him with nothing, Willy feels an acute need to put his sons—especially Biff—on the right path in life. He convinces himself that he is capable of doing so, which leads to his inflated sense of self-importance (as when he tells his young sons about how well known he is in New England). Willy's ultimate belief in the deluded prospect of Biff's imminent success causes him to trade in his own life to leave Biff $20,000. As an additional consequence of being abandoned, Willy knows little about his father and thus has to ask Ben to tell Biff and Happy about their grandfather.

Willy's fear of abandonment is probably also responsible for his obsession with being well liked. Somewhat childlike, Willy craves approval and reacts to any perceived hint of dislike by either throwing a tantrum or retreating into self-pity. When Ben visits Willy's home, Willy proudly shows his sons to Ben, practically begging for a word of approval. When Ben notes that he has to leave to catch his train, Willy begs him to stay a little longer. Even as an adult, Willy's relationship to Ben is fraught with this fear of abandonment. Howard abandons Willy by firing him, and after Happy and Biff abandon him in the restaurant, Willy returns home like a dejected child. After these blows, the power of Willy's fantasies to deny unpleasant facts about his reality abandons him as well.

3. *Willy and Biff have different explanations for Biff's failure to succeed in the business world. How are their explanations different?*

Willy believes that Biff's discovery of Willy's adulterous affair contributed to Biff's disillusionment with the American Dream that Willy cherishes so dearly. He remembers that Biff called him a "phony little fake." Essentially, Willy interprets Biff's words to mean that Biff thinks of him as a charlatan: Willy believes that his affair prevented him from selling Biff on the American Dream. On the other hand, Biff believes that he failed to succeed in business precisely because Willy sold him so successfully on the American Dream of easy success. By the time he took his first job, Biff was so convinced that success would inevitably fall into his lap that he was unwilling to work hard in order to advance to more important positions. Biff did not want to start at the bottom and deal with taking orders. He had faith in Willy's prediction that he was naturally destined to move ahead, so he made no efforts to do so through hard work, and, as a result, he failed miserably.

STUDY QUESTIONS

How to Write
Literary Analysis

The Literary Essay: A Step-by-Step Guide

When you read for pleasure, your only goal is enjoyment. You might find yourself reading to get caught up in an exciting story, to learn about an interesting time or place, or just to pass time. Maybe you're looking for inspiration, guidance, or a reflection of your own life. There are as many different, valid ways of reading a book as there are books in the world.

When you read a work of literature in an English class, however, you're being asked to read in a special way: you're being asked to perform *literary analysis*. To analyze something means to break it down into smaller parts and then examine how those parts work, both individually and together. Literary analysis involves examining all the parts of a novel, play, short story, or poem—elements such as character, setting, tone, and imagery—and thinking about how the author uses those elements to create certain effects.

A literary essay isn't a book review: you're not being asked whether or not you liked a book or whether you'd recommend it to another reader. A literary essay also isn't like the kind of book report you wrote when you were younger, where your teacher wanted you to summarize the book's action. A high school- or college-level literary essay asks, "How does this piece of literature actually work?" "How does it do what it does?" and, "Why might the author have made the choices he or she did?"

The Seven Steps
No one is born knowing how to analyze literature; it's a skill you learn and a process you can master. As you gain more practice with this kind of thinking and writing, you'll be able to craft a method that works best for you. But until then, here are seven basic steps to writing a well-constructed literary essay:

1. *Ask questions*
2. *Collect evidence*
3. *Construct a thesis*

53

4. Develop and organize arguments
5. Write the introduction
6. Write the body paragraphs
7. Write the conclusion

---

1. ASK QUESTIONS

When you're assigned a literary essay in class, your teacher will often provide you with a list of writing prompts. Lucky you! Now all you have to do is choose one. Do yourself a favor and pick a topic that interests you. You'll have a much better (not to mention easier) time if you start off with something you enjoy thinking about. If you are asked to come up with a topic by yourself, though, you might start to feel a little panicked. Maybe you have too many ideas—or none at all. Don't worry. Take a deep breath and start by asking yourself these questions:

- **What struck you?** Did a particular image, line, or scene linger in your mind for a long time? If it fascinated you, chances are you can draw on it to write a fascinating essay.

- **What confused you?** Maybe you were surprised to see a character act in a certain way, or maybe you didn't understand why the book ended the way it did. Confusing moments in a work of literature are like a loose thread in a sweater: if you pull on it, you can unravel the entire thing. Ask yourself why the author chose to write about that character or scene the way he or she did and you might tap into some important insights about the work as a whole.

- **Did you notice any patterns?** Is there a phrase that the main character uses constantly or an image that repeats throughout the book? If you can figure out how that pattern weaves through the work and what the significance of that pattern is, you've almost got your entire essay mapped out.

- **Did you notice any contradictions or ironies?** Great works of literature are complex; great literary essays recognize and explain those complexities. Maybe the title (*Happy Days*) totally disagrees with the book's subject matter (hungry orphans dying in the woods). Maybe the main character acts one way around his family and a completely different way around his friends and associates. If you can find a way to explain a work's contradictory elements, you've got the seeds of a great essay.

At this point, you don't need to know exactly what you're going to say about your topic; you just need a place to begin your exploration. You can help direct your reading and brainstorming by formulating your topic as a *question*, which you'll then try to answer in your essay. The best questions invite critical debates and discussions, not just a rehashing of the summary. Remember, you're looking for something you can *prove or argue* based on evidence you find in the text. Finally, remember to keep the scope of your question in mind: is this a topic you can adequately address within the word or page limit you've been given? Conversely, is this a topic big enough to fill the required length?

GOOD QUESTIONS
"Are Romeo and Juliet's parents responsible for the deaths of their children?"
"Why do pigs keep showing up in LORD OF THE FLIES*?"*
"Are Dr. Frankenstein and his monster alike? How?"

BAD QUESTIONS
"What happens to Scout in TO KILL A MOCKINGBIRD*?"*
"What do the other characters in JULIUS CAESAR *think about Caesar?"*
"How does Hester Prynne in THE SCARLET LETTER *remind me of my sister?"*

---

2. COLLECT EVIDENCE
Once you know what question you want to answer, it's time to scour the book for things that will help you answer the question. Don't worry if you don't know what you want to say yet—right now you're just collecting ideas and material and letting it all percolate. Keep track of passages, symbols, images, or scenes that deal with your topic. Eventually, you'll start making connections between these examples and your thesis will emerge.

Here's a brief summary of the various parts that compose each and every work of literature. These are the elements that you will analyze in your essay, and which you will offer as evidence to support your arguments. For more on the parts of literary works, see the Glossary of Literary Terms at the end of this section.

ELEMENTS OF STORY   These are the *what*s of the work—what happens, where it happens, and to whom it happens.

- **Plot:** All of the events and actions of the work.

- **Character:** The people who act and are acted upon in a literary work. The main character of a work is known as the *protagonist.*

- **Conflict:** The central tension in the work. In most cases, the protagonist wants something, while opposing forces (antagonists) hinder the protagonist's progress.

- **Setting:** When and where the work takes place. Elements of setting include location, time period, time of day, weather, social atmosphere, and economic conditions.

- **Narrator:** The person telling the story. The narrator may straightforwardly report what happens, convey the subjective opinions and perceptions of one or more characters, or provide commentary and opinion in his or her own voice.

- **Themes:** The main idea or message of the work—usually an abstract idea about people, society, or life in general. A work may have many themes, which may be in tension with one another.

ELEMENTS OF STYLE   These are the *how*s—how the characters speak, how the story is constructed, and how language is used throughout the work.

- **Structure and organization:** How the parts of the work are assembled. Some novels are narrated in a linear, chronological fashion, while others skip around in time. Some plays follow a traditional three- or five-act structure, while others are a series of loosely connected scenes. Some authors deliberately leave gaps in their works, leaving readers to puzzle out the missing information. A work's structure and organization can tell you a lot about the kind of message it wants to convey.

- **Point of view:** The perspective from which a story is told. In *first-person point of view,* the narrator involves him or herself in the story. ("I went to the store"; "We watched in horror as the bird slammed into the window.") A first-person narrator is usually the protagonist of the work, but not always. In *third-person point of view,* the narrator does not participate

in the story. A third-person narrator may closely follow a specific character, recounting that individual character's thoughts or experiences, or it may be what we call an *omniscient* narrator. Omniscient narrators see and know all: they can witness any event in any time or place and are privy to the inner thoughts and feelings of all characters. Remember that the narrator and the author are not the same thing!

- **Diction:** Word choice. Whether a character uses dry, clinical language or flowery prose with lots of exclamation points can tell you a lot about his or her attitude and personality.

- **Syntax:** Word order and sentence construction. Syntax is a crucial part of establishing an author's narrative voice. Ernest Hemingway, for example, is known for writing in very short, straightforward sentences, while James Joyce characteristically wrote in long, incredibly complicated lines.

- **Tone:** The mood or feeling of the text. Diction and syntax often contribute to the tone of a work. A novel written in short, clipped sentences that use small, simple words might feel brusque, cold, or matter-of-fact.

- **Imagery:** Language that appeals to the senses, representing things that can be seen, smelled, heard, tasted, or touched.

- **Figurative language:** Language that is not meant to be interpreted literally. The most common types of figurative language are *metaphors* and *similes*, which compare two unlike things in order to suggest a similarity between them—for example, "All the world's a stage," or "The moon is like a ball of green cheese." (Metaphors say one thing *is* another thing; similes claim that one thing is *like* another thing.)

---

3. CONSTRUCT A THESIS

When you've examined all the evidence you've collected and know how you want to answer the question, it's time to write your thesis statement. A *thesis* is a claim about a work of literature that needs to be supported by evidence and arguments. The thesis statement is the heart of the literary essay, and the bulk of your paper will be spent trying to prove this claim. A good thesis will be:

- **Arguable.** "*The Great Gatsby* describes New York society in the 1920s" isn't a thesis—it's a fact.

- **Provable through textual evidence.** *"Hamlet* is a confusing but ultimately very well-written play" is a weak thesis because it offers the writer's personal opinion about the book. Yes, it's arguable, but it's not a claim that can be proved or supported with examples taken from the play itself.

- **Surprising.** "Both George and Lenny change a great deal in *Of Mice and Men"* is a weak thesis because it's obvious. A really strong thesis will argue for a reading of the text that is not immediately apparent.

- **Specific.** "Dr. Frankenstein's monster tells us a lot about the human condition" is *almost* a really great thesis statement, but it's still too vague. What does the writer mean by "a lot"? *How* does the monster tell us so much about the human condition?

GOOD THESIS STATEMENTS

Question: In *Romeo and Juliet,* which is more powerful in shaping the lovers' story: fate or foolishness?

Thesis: "Though Shakespeare defines Romeo and Juliet as 'star-crossed lovers' and images of stars and planets appear throughout the play, a closer examination of that celestial imagery reveals that the stars are merely witnesses to the characters' foolish activities and not the causes themselves."

Question: How does the bell jar function as a symbol in Sylvia Plath's *The Bell Jar?*

Thesis: "A bell jar is a bell-shaped glass that has three basic uses: to hold a specimen for observation, to contain gases, and to maintain a vacuum. The bell jar appears in each of these capacities in *The Bell Jar,* Plath's semi-autobiographical novel, and each appearance marks a different stage in Esther's mental breakdown."

Question: Would Piggy in *The Lord of the Flies* make a good island leader if he were given the chance?

Thesis: "Though the intelligent, rational, and innovative Piggy has the mental characteristics of a good leader, he ultimately lacks the social skills necessary to be an effective one. Golding emphasizes this point by giving Piggy a foil in the charismatic Jack, whose magnetic personality allows him to capture and wield power effectively, if not always wisely."

4. DEVELOP AND ORGANIZE ARGUMENTS

The reasons and examples that support your thesis will form the middle paragraphs of your essay. Since you can't really write your thesis statement until you know how you'll structure your argument, you'll probably end up working on steps 3 and 4 at the same time.

There's no single method of argumentation that will work in every context. One essay prompt might ask you to compare and contrast two characters, while another asks you to trace an image through a given work of literature. These questions require different kinds of answers and therefore different kinds of arguments. Below, we'll discuss three common kinds of essay prompts and some strategies for constructing a solid, well-argued case.

TYPES OF LITERARY ESSAYS

- **Compare and contrast**

  Compare and contrast the characters of Huck and Jim in THE ADVENTURES OF HUCKLEBERRY FINN.

  Chances are you've written this kind of essay before. In an academic literary context, you'll organize your arguments the same way you would in any other class. You can either go *subject by subject* or *point by point*. In the former, you'll discuss one character first and then the second. In the latter, you'll choose several traits (attitude toward life, social status, images and metaphors associated with the character) and devote a paragraph to each. You may want to use a mix of these two approaches—for example, you may want to spend a paragraph a piece broadly sketching Huck's and Jim's personalities before transitioning into a paragraph or two that describes a few key points of comparison. This can be a highly effective strategy if you want to make a counterintuitive argument—that, despite seeming to be totally different, the two objects being compared are actually similar in a very important way (or vice versa). Remember that your essay should reveal something fresh or unexpected about the text, so think beyond the obvious parallels and differences.

- **Trace**

  Choose an image—for example, birds, knives, or eyes—and trace that image throughout MACBETH.

  Sounds pretty easy, right? All you need to do is read the play, underline every appearance of a knife in *Macbeth,* and then list

LITERARY ANALYSIS

them in your essay in the order they appear, right? Well, not exactly. Your teacher doesn't want a simple catalog of examples. He or she wants to see you make *connections* between those examples—that's the difference between summarizing and analyzing. In the *Macbeth* example above, think about the different contexts in which knives appear in the play and to what effect. In *Macbeth*, there are real knives and imagined knives; knives that kill and knives that simply threaten. Categorize and classify your examples to give them some order. Finally, always keep the overall effect in mind. After you choose and analyze your examples, you should come to some greater understanding about the work, as well as your chosen image, symbol, or phrase's role in developing the major themes and stylistic strategies of that work.

- **Debate**

  Is the society depicted in 1984 *good for its citizens?*

  In this kind of essay, you're being asked to debate a moral, ethical, or aesthetic issue regarding the work. You might be asked to judge a character or group of characters (*Is Caesar responsible for his own demise?*) or the work itself (*Is* JANE EYRE *a feminist novel?*). For this kind of essay, there are two important points to keep in mind. First, don't simply base your arguments on your personal feelings and reactions. Every literary essay expects you to read and analyze the work, so search for evidence in the text. What do characters in *1984* have to say about the government of Oceania? What images does Orwell use that might give you a hint about his attitude toward the government? As in any debate, you also need to make sure that you define all the necessary terms before you begin to argue your case. What does it mean to be a "good" society? What makes a novel "feminist"? You should define your terms right up front, in the first paragraph after your introduction.

  Second, remember that strong literary essays make contrary and surprising arguments. Try to think outside the box. In the *1984* example above, it seems like the obvious answer would be no, the totalitarian society depicted in Orwell's novel is *not* good for its citizens. But can you think of any arguments for the opposite side? Even if your final assertion is that the novel depicts a cruel, repressive, and therefore harmful society, acknowledging and responding to the counterargument will strengthen your overall case.

5. WRITE THE INTRODUCTION

Your introduction sets up the entire essay. It's where you present your topic and articulate the particular issues and questions you'll be addressing. It's also where you, as the writer, introduce yourself to your readers. A persuasive literary essay immediately establishes its writer as a knowledgeable, authoritative figure.

An introduction can vary in length depending on the overall length of the essay, but in a traditional five-paragraph essay it should be no longer than one paragraph. However long it is, your introduction needs to:

- **Provide any necessary context.** Your introduction should situate the reader and let him or her know what to expect. What book are you discussing? Which characters? What topic will you be addressing?

- **Answer the "So what?" question.** Why is this topic important, and why is your particular position on the topic noteworthy? Ideally, your introduction should pique the reader's interest by suggesting how your argument is surprising or otherwise counterintuitive. Literary essays make unexpected connections and reveal less-than-obvious truths.

- **Present your thesis.** This usually happens at or very near the end of your introduction.

- **Indicate the shape of the essay to come.** Your reader should finish reading your introduction with a good sense of the scope of your essay as well as the path you'll take toward proving your thesis. You don't need to spell out every step, but you do need to suggest the organizational pattern you'll be using.

Your introduction should not:

- **Be vague.** Beware of the two killer words in literary analysis: *interesting* and *important*. Of course the work, question, or example is interesting and important—that's why you're writing about it!

- **Open with any grandiose assertions.** Many student readers think that beginning their essays with a flamboyant statement such as, "Since the dawn of time, writers have been fascinated with the topic of free will," makes them sound important and commanding. You know what? It actually sounds pretty amateurish.

- **Wildly praise the work.** Another typical mistake student writers make is extolling the work or author. Your teacher doesn't need to be told that "Shakespeare is perhaps the greatest writer in the English language." You can mention a work's reputation in passing—by referring to *The Adventures of Huckleberry Finn* as "Mark Twain's enduring classic," for example—but don't make a point of bringing it up unless that reputation is key to your argument.

- **Go off-topic.** Keep your introduction streamlined and to the point. Don't feel the need to throw in all kinds of bells and whistles in order to impress your reader—just get to the point as quickly as you can, without skimping on any of the required steps.

---

6. Write the Body Paragraphs

Once you've written your introduction, you'll take the arguments you developed in step 4 and turn them into your body paragraphs. The organization of this middle section of your essay will largely be determined by the argumentative strategy you use, but no matter how you arrange your thoughts, your body paragraphs need to do the following:

- **Begin with a strong topic sentence.** Topic sentences are like signs on a highway: they tell the reader where they are and where they're going. A good topic sentence not only alerts readers to what issue will be discussed in the following paragraph but also gives them a sense of what argument will be made *about* that issue. "Rumor and gossip play an important role in *The Crucible*" isn't a strong topic sentence because it doesn't tell us very much. "The community's constant gossiping creates an environment that allows false accusations to flourish" is a much stronger topic sentence— it not only tells us *what* the paragraph will discuss (gossip) but *how* the paragraph will discuss the topic (by showing how gossip creates a set of conditions that leads to the play's climactic action).

- **Fully and completely develop a single thought.** Don't skip around in your paragraph or try to stuff in too much material. Body paragraphs are like bricks: each individual one needs to be strong and sturdy or the entire structure will collapse. Make sure you have really proven your point before moving on to the next one.

- **Use transitions effectively.** Good literary essay writers know that each paragraph must be clearly and strongly linked to the material around it. Think of each paragraph as a response to the one that precedes it. Use transition words and phrases such as *however, similarly, on the contrary, therefore,* and *furthermore* to indicate what kind of response you're making.

---

7. WRITE THE CONCLUSION

Just as you used the introduction to ground your readers in the topic before providing your thesis, you'll use the conclusion to quickly summarize the specifics learned thus far and then hint at the broader implications of your topic. A good conclusion will:

- **Do more than simply restate the thesis.** If your thesis argued that *The Catcher in the Rye* can be read as a Christian allegory, don't simply end your essay by saying, "And that is why *The Catcher in the Rye* can be read as a Christian allegory." If you've constructed your arguments well, this kind of statement will just be redundant.

- **Synthesize the arguments, not summarize them.** Similarly, don't repeat the details of your body paragraphs in your conclusion. The reader has already read your essay, and chances are it's not so long that they've forgotten all your points by now.

- **Revisit the "So what?" question.** In your introduction, you made a case for why your topic and position are important. You should close your essay with the same sort of gesture. What do your readers know now that they didn't know before? How will that knowledge help them better appreciate or understand the work overall?

- **Move from the specific to the general.** Your essay has most likely treated a very specific element of the work—a single character, a small set of images, or a particular passage. In your conclusion, try to show how this narrow discussion has wider implications for the work overall. If your essay on *To Kill a Mockingbird* focused on the character of Boo Radley, for example, you might want to include a bit in your conclusion about how he fits into the novel's larger message about childhood, innocence, or family life.

- **Stay relevant.** Your conclusion should suggest new directions of thought, but it shouldn't be treated as an opportunity to pad your essay with all the extra, interesting ideas you came up with during your brainstorming sessions but couldn't fit into the essay proper. Don't attempt to stuff in unrelated queries or too many abstract thoughts.

- **Avoid making overblown closing statements.** A conclusion should open up your highly specific, focused discussion, but it should do so without drawing a sweeping lesson about life or human nature. Making such observations may be part of the point of reading, but it's almost always a mistake in essays, where these observations tend to sound overly dramatic or simply silly.

A+ Essay Checklist

Congratulations! If you've followed all the steps we've outlined above, you should have a solid literary essay to show for all your efforts. What if you've got your sights set on an A+? To write the kind of superlative essay that will be rewarded with a perfect grade, keep the following rubric in mind. These are the qualities that teachers expect to see in a truly A+ essay. How does yours stack up?

- ✓ Demonstrates a thorough understanding of the book
- ✓ Presents an original, compelling argument
- ✓ Thoughtfully analyzes the text's formal elements
- ✓ Uses appropriate and insightful examples
- ✓ Structures ideas in a logical and progressive order
- ✓ Demonstrates a mastery of sentence construction, transitions, grammar, spelling, and word choice

SUGGESTED ESSAY TOPICS

1. *Willy recalls his sons' teenage years as an idyllic past. What evidence can we find to show that the past is not as idyllic as Willy imagines it to be?*

2. *What evidence can we find to show that Willy may have chosen a profession that is at odds with his natural inclinations?*

3. *Why does Willy reject Charley's job offer?*

4. *How does Willy's interview with Howard reveal that Willy transfers his professional anxieties onto his relationship with his family and conflates the professional and personal realms of his life?*

5. *What evidence can we find to show that Willy misses the distinction between being loved and being well liked? What are the consequences of Willy's failure to distinguish between the two?*

6. *How does Willy's desperate quest for the American Dream resemble a religious crusade?*

A+ Student Essay

> Willy Loman is constantly reminiscing and thinking
> about the past. Why? What effect does this have on him
> and on the play?

To an unusual degree, *The Death of a Salesman* interweaves past and present action. Willy Loman, the play's protagonist, repeatedly revisits old memories, sometimes even conflating them with the present moment. But these memories are not the sentimental, slightly melancholy daydreams of a contented man. Instead, they are the dark clues to Willy's present state of mental and emotional disrepair. Miller uses the extended flashbacks to show both that Willy longs to understand himself, and also that his efforts to do so are doomed.

Willy revisits the past not in an effort to sink into happy memories, but in an effort to analyze himself and understand where his life went wrong. His flashbacks are hardly comforting flights into idealized past times. Rather, they are harrowing journeys that get to the heart of his dysfunction. When Willy thinks about the old days, he remembers making light of Biff's thieving, barking at Linda about the state of her stockings, ignoring Biff's mistreatment of young women, sidelining Happy, and so on. Each of these memories lays bare one of Willy's shortcomings: his failure to instill strong morals in his sons, his guilt over his adultery, his inability to see Biff objectively, and his unequal love for Biff and Happy, respectively. If Willy's dips into the past were purely escapist, he would fixate on the happy moments in his life. Instead, he tends to be drawn to the times at which he behaved in revealingly unpleasant ways. This tendency suggests that Willy longs for self-knowledge. He wants to figure out how he got into his present mess, and he knows that the answers lie in the past.

Paradoxically, the very strength of Willy's impulse to understand himself scuttles his efforts at gaining self-knowledge. In his ineffectual desperation to understand what went wrong, he becomes subsumed by the past. Instead of remaining firmly rooted in the present and thinking about how the past applies to the life he is now living, he pulls his memories over his head like a blanket. Miller brings this absorption to life by fully dramatizing Willy's flashbacks.

They are not narrated in the first person or addressed to the audience, as might befit events that occurred in the past and are at a remove. Rather, they are played out as fully realized scenes, just as vital and urgent as the present-day scenes are. By dramatizing Willy's memories, Miller makes them as vivid for us as they are for Willy. Miller suggests that while Willy might benefit from sticking a toe into the waters of the past, he begins to lose his grip on sanity when he plunges in those waters completely.

Willy's efforts at self-analysis are doomed not just because he gives himself wholly to his memories, but also because his passionate emotions are not balanced by cool critical thinking. Willy is constitutionally incapable of analyzing his own behavior, understanding his character, and comprehending the mistakes he has made. Over and over, Miller shows how Willy plunges back into the past, stares uncomprehendingly at the errors he made, and then makes those identical errors in the present. He remembers idealizing Ben as a boy; then he describes Ben in outsized, glowing terms to his sons. He remembers implying that Biff did not need to work hard in order to attend a good college; then he bridles at the implication that his parenting has something to do with Biff's failure. Willy dimly senses that his past missteps have a bearing on the present, but he cannot bring himself to make the connections explicit.

Willy Loman has a multitude of faults, but escapism is not one of them. He truly wants to understand himself; part of his tragedy is that he is incapable of doing so.

GLOSSARY OF LITERARY TERMS

ANTAGONIST

The entity that acts to frustrate the goals of the *protagonist*. The antagonist is usually another *character* but may also be a non-human force.

ANTIHERO / ANTIHEROINE

A *protagonist* who is not admirable or who challenges notions of what should be considered admirable.

CHARACTER

A person, animal, or any other thing with a personality that appears in a *narrative*.

CLIMAX

The moment of greatest intensity in a text or the major turning point in the *plot*.

CONFLICT

The central struggle that moves the *plot* forward. The conflict can be the *protagonist*'s struggle against fate, nature, society, or another person.

FIRST-PERSON POINT OF VIEW

A literary style in which the *narrator* tells the story from his or her own *point of view* and refers to himself or herself as "I." The narrator may be an active participant in the story or just an observer.

HERO / HEROINE

The principal *character* in a literary work or *narrative*.

IMAGERY

Language that brings to mind sense-impressions, representing things that can be seen, smelled, heard, tasted, or touched.

MOTIF

A recurring idea, structure, contrast, or device that develops or informs the major *themes* of a work of literature.

NARRATIVE

A story.

NARRATOR

The person (sometimes a *character*) who tells a story; the *voice* assumed by the writer. The narrator and the author of the work of literature are not the same person.

PLOT

The arrangement of the events in a story, including the sequence in which they are told, the relative emphasis they are given, and the causal connections between events.

POINT OF VIEW

The *perspective* that a *narrative* takes toward the events it describes.

PROTAGONIST

The main *character* around whom the story revolves.

SETTING

The location of a *narrative* in time and space. Setting creates mood or atmosphere.

SUBPLOT

A secondary *plot* that is of less importance to the overall story but may serve as a point of contrast or comparison to the main plot.

SYMBOL

An object, *character,* figure, or color that is used to represent an abstract idea or concept. Unlike an *emblem,* a symbol may have different meanings in different contexts.

SYNTAX

The way the words in a piece of writing are put together to form lines, phrases, or clauses; the basic structure of a piece of writing.

THEME

A fundamental and universal idea explored in a literary work.

TONE

The author's attitude toward the subject or *characters* of a story or poem or toward the reader.

VOICE

An author's individual way of using language to reflect his or her own personality and attitudes. An author communicates voice through *tone, diction,* and *syntax.*

LITERARY ANALYSIS

A Note on Plagiarism

Plagiarism—presenting someone else's work as your own—rears its ugly head in many forms. Many students know that copying text without citing it is unacceptable. But some don't realize that even if you're not quoting directly, but instead are paraphrasing or summarizing, *it is plagiarism* unless you cite the source.

Here are the most common forms of plagiarism:

- Using an author's phrases, sentences, or paragraphs without citing the source
- Paraphrasing an author's ideas without citing the source
- Passing off another student's work as your own

How do you steer clear of plagiarism? You should *always* acknowledge all words and ideas that aren't your own by using quotation marks around verbatim text or citations like footnotes and endnotes to note another writer's ideas. For more information on how to give credit when credit is due, ask your teacher for guidance or visit www.sparknotes.com.

REVIEW & RESOURCES

QUIZ

1. What was Biff doing in the West before the play begins?

    A. Laying railroad tracks
    B. Selling dishwashers
    C. Working on a farm
    D. Robbing banks

2. What did Biff steal from Bill Oliver's store when he was a boy?

    A. A crate of basketballs
    B. A wire recorder
    C. A suit
    D. A car

3. What does Biff steal from Bill Oliver's office as an adult?

    A. A trophy
    B. Seeds
    C. Money
    D. A pen

4. What product does Willy sell?

    A. Bibles
    B. Appliances
    C. Sporting goods
    D. Miller doesn't specify

5. For what region is Willy responsible in his sales?

    A. New England
    B. Brooklyn
    C. Queens and Long Island
    D. New Jersey

6. How old is Happy?

   A. 34
   B. 28
   C. 32
   D. 30

7. What did Willy's father sell?

   A. Flutes
   B. Dictionaries
   C. Pizzas
   D. False teeth

8. Where did Willy's father go after he abandoned his family?

   A. Alabama
   B. Spain
   C. Alaska
   D. Las Vegas

9. Where did Ben end up when he went looking for his father?

   A. Africa
   B. Alaska
   C. Brooklyn
   D. Boston

10. Where does Biff find Willy with The Woman?

    A. Manhattan
    B. Hartford
    C. Providence
    D. Boston

11. How old was Dave Singleman when he died?

    A. 63
    B. 84
    C. 74
    D. 59

12. What is the name of the restaurant where Happy and Biff take Willy?

    A. Frank's Chop House
    B. Sam's Hoagie Shack
    C. Divine Seafood
    D. The Carnage Deli

13. How much money does Charley usually give Willy each week?

    A. $150
    B. $75
    C. $200
    D. $50

14. What subject did Biff fail in high school?

    A. Math
    B. English
    C. Physics
    D. History

15. Where does Happy work?

    A. In a factory
    B. In a store
    C. At a restaurant
    D. On Wall Street

16. What was Biff's position at Bill Oliver's store when he was a boy?

    A. Salesman
    B. Manager
    C. Window dresser
    D. Shipping clerk

17. On what day of the week does Willy die?

    A. Saturday
    B. Sunday
    C. Tuesday
    D. Monday

REVIEW & RESOURCES

18. On the sales trip that immediately precedes the beginning of the play, which city did Willy reach before turning back?

    A. Boston
    B. Hartford
    C. Buffalo
    D. Yonkers

19. How long has Willy worked for his sales firm?

    A. Between thirty-four and thirty-six years
    B. Thirty-two years
    C. Forty years
    D. Twenty-five years

20. What does Howard show Willy in his office?

    A. His pen
    B. His typewriter
    C. His wire recorder
    D. A picture of his family

21. What is Bernard's adult occupation?

    A. Police officer
    B. Lawyer
    C. Doctor
    D. Writer

22. What does Biff allow Bernard to carry to the Ebbets Field game?

    A. His helmet
    B. His football
    C. His cleats
    D. His shoulder pads

23. What is the name of Charley's secretary?

    A. Michelle
    B. Jill
    C. Jenny
    D. Angela

24. What does Happy order from Stanley at the restaurant?

    A. Lobsters
    B. Steak
    C. Veal
    D. Red snapper

25. To what kind of store does Willy ask Stanley to direct him?

    A. A deli
    B. A shoe store
    C. A sporting goods store
    D. A seed store

Suggestions for Further Reading

BIGSBY, CHRISTOPHER, ed. *The Cambridge Companion to Arthur Miller*. New York: Cambridge University Press, 1997.

BLOOM, HAROLD, ed. *Arthur Miller: Modern Critical Views*. New York: Chelsea House Publishing, 1988.

BLOOM, HAROLD, ed. *Arthur Miller's* DEATH OF A SALESMAN: *Modern Critical Interpretations*. New York: Chelsea House Publishing, 2006.

MARTIN, ROBERT A., and STEVEN R. CENTOLA, eds. *The Theater Essays of Arthur Miller*. New York: Da Capo Press, 2nd edition 2001.

MILLER, ARTHUR. *Timebends: A Life*. New York: Penguin USA, reprint edition 1995.

MURPHY, BRENDA. *Death of a Salesman*. New York: Cambridge University Press, reprint edition 2005.

SARTRE, JEAN-PAUL. *Being and Nothingness: A Phenomenological Essay on Ontology*. New York: Washington Square Press, 1993.

SIEBOLD, THOMAS, ed. *Readings on* DEATH OF A SALESMAN. San Diego, CA: Greenhaven Press, 1998.

REVIEW & RESOURCES